How to Write a Children's Picture Book

How to Write a Children's Picture Book

Learning from
The Very Hungry Caterpillar,
Chicka Chicka Boom Boom,
Corduroy,
Where the Wild Things Are,
The Carrot Seed,
Good Night, Gorilla,
Sylvester and the Magic Pebble,
and Other Favorite Stories

Eve Heidi Bine-Stock

E & E Publishing
Sausalito, California

E & E Publishing
1001 Bridgeway, No. 227
Sausalito, California 94965
U.S.A.
Website: www.EandEGroup.com/Publishing
Email: EandEGroup@EandEGroup.com

Publisher's Cataloging In Publication
(Prepared by The Donohue Group, Inc.)

Bine-Stock, Eve Heidi.

    How to write a children's picture book : learning from The very hungry caterpillar ... and other favorite stories / Eve Heidi Bine-Stock.

        p. : ill. ; cm.
        ISBN: 0-9719898-8-5

1. Picture books for children--Technique. 2. Picture books for children--Authorship. 3. Authorship. I. Title.

PN147.5 .B56 2004
808/.06/8

Printed in U.S.A.

Acknowledgments

Thank you to Susan Hicks for her good-natured and professional proofreading.

Special thanks to Melanie Abel for her creativity and generosity in writing stories especially for this volume to illustrate various points I was making about story structure.

And most important, heartfelt thanks to my husband, Edward, who endured loneliness and hunger and heated debate while I wrote this book—and insists that it was worth it! His sensitivity and insight into literary criticism, as well as his unwavering professionalism, helped me immeasurably in crafting this work.

Contents

Acknowledgments...5

Introduction 9

Part I

The Very Hungry Caterpillar......................... 17

Freight Train.......................................19

Ten, Nine, Eight 23

Chicka Chicka Boom Boom...........................25

I am a Bunny.......................................27

Goodnight Moon 31

The Carrot Seed 35

Seven Blind Mice 43

"The Tub" from *George and Martha* 47

Farmer Duck 53

If You Give a Mouse a Cookie.....................55

The Snowy Day 59

Part II

Picture Storybooks: The Symmetrical Paradigm .65

Leo the Late Bloomer 79

Harry the Dirty Dog 85

Corduroy 91

Good Night, Gorilla...............................97

Sylvester and the Magic Pebble....................103

Strega Nona *109*

Stone Soup *115*

Make Way for Ducklings *121*

Where the Wild Things Are...................... *127*

Madeline.. *133*

Miss Nelson is Missing! *141*

Owen.. *147*

"The Letter" from *Frog and Toad are Friends*...*151*

Part III

Picture Storybooks: The Iterative Paradigm *157*

Mike Mulligan and His Steam Shovel............ *161*

Millions of Cats *167*

Part IV

Preparing to Write the Picture Storybook *175*

Appendix *193*

Bibliography *197*

Index *201*

About the Author *203*

Introduction

For this exploration into what makes a successful children's picture book, I wanted to choose the most beloved, time-tested, reader-tested books.

Therefore, I selected books from the list *100 Pictures Books Everyone Should Know* compiled by the New York City Public Library and from a collection entitled *The 20th Century Children's Book Treasury,* selected by Janet Schulman.

All of the children's picture books discussed in this volume are consequently readily available for anyone to acquire and study.

Types of Picture Books

In Part I of this volume, we analyze favorite concept books: alphabet books, counting books, naming books, and books that explore an idea, object or activity.

In Parts II and III, we analyze celebrated picture storybooks. These have a simple plot—usually involving a problem that the main character must overcome—and engaging pictures that tell part of the story.

Structure: The Key to Writing a Picture Book

There is a lot to consider when writing a children's picture book: tone, word choice, plot, character, setting, theme, style, and so on. There are many books and articles that discuss these elements of a children's picture book.

This volume, however, emphasizes an aspect of picture books that, ironically, has not yet been thoroughly investigated: _structure._

Both concept books and picture story-books employ very distinctive structures that, once mastered, can be applied to any picture book you wish to write.

Think of structure as a hanger. It holds and shapes an infinite variety of shirts, blouses, dresses, coats and suits. In the same way, picture book _structures_ can hold and shape an endless variety of concept books and picture storybooks.

It does not matter what the theme is, what the plot is, or who the characters are; these structures give shape to the world's favorite picture books, and they will help you to write your own successful picture books, as well.

One of the most important structures you will learn about is the Symmetrical Picture Storybook Paradigm. This is the structure which underlies most of the best-loved picture storybooks.

The celebrated authors who wrote these books were certainly not aware of this paradigm and never called it by name. But their intuition led them to create stories with the same underlying structure, which I call the Symmetrical Picture Storybook Paradigm.

When so many of the best picture storybooks employ the same structure, it is important to analyze that structure, understand why it works, and learn how to incorporate it into your own writing. This volume helps you do all that.

You will see that no matter how carefully you labor over the tone, word choice, plot, character, setting, theme and style of your picture book, you must have a thorough grasp of its *structure* if you wish your book to succeed.

Indeed, you will find that an expert command of *structure* is the key to writing a successful children's picture book.

Please note that before you read about specific picture storybooks in Part II, it will be helpful to you if you first read the introduction to Part II, entitled "Picture Storybooks: The Symmetrical Paradigm."

Other Salient Features of Picture Books

Part I of this volume also explores what the best-loved picture books can teach us about:

- irony
- anthropomorphism
- pacing
- the interplay of text and picture
- cause-and-effect in plots
- the difference in emotional response to climactic vs. episodic plots
- the effect of using the present tense
- the effect of showing character through action

By learning how the best writers incorporate these features into favorite picture books, you can apply similar successful techniques in your own writing.

Preparing to Write Your Own Picture Storybook

Part IV of this volume guides you step-by-step through the process of preparing to write your own picture storybook.

Like an architect who draws a blueprint before starting to build, a writer should plan his story before sitting down to actually write it.

Part IV holds your hand and guides you through this process, so that you will have the entire plot and *structure* of your story well thought out before you write even one word of your story.

Follow the steps in Part IV and you will have the "road map" of your story. Secure in the knowledge that you know where your story is going, you will be able to write with confidence.

Part I

The Very Hungry Caterpillar

by Eric Carle

In this story of a tiny, hungry caterpillar on an eating spree, the physical pages of the book themselves participate in telling the story every bit as much as the words and pictures do.

Each day, the size of the page grows to accommodate yet another piece of food.

And as the caterpillar munches through a piece of food, he munches through the page, too: as he exits the food, he comes through the verso!

The story surprises us, too: on Saturday, we expect to see six pieces of respectable fruit—but get *ten* pieces of outrageous junk food! We hold our bellies with laughter—and a bit of queasiness from all that bingeing!

The exaggeration playfully teaches us an important lesson: a caterpillar needs energy from food to transform into a butterfly.

Finally, the structure of this story is like the caterpillar himself: a Beginning, an End and a *l-o-n-g* Middle.

As you can see from *The Very Hungry Caterpillar*, the children's book writer needs not only a great imagination, but a publisher with vision as well.

Freight Train

by Donald Crews

This book starts with an empty track and a mystery: What is a freight train?

We find out, "clue" by "clue," railcar by railcar, and only after we've seen all the "clues" do we see the whole train.

That makes up the first half of the book.

The second half is all about the *movement* of the train: *Where* does it move? *When* does it move?

Finally, as the train passes by, we end up where we started: with an empty track.

So you see, this book has the simple two-part structure common to books for toddlers and creates a satisfying circle by both starting and ending with an empty track.

But wait! There's more.

Let us take a closer look at each half. You will see that each half has a beginning, middle and end—the classic three-part structure used in stories throughout the ages because it is so *satisfying*.

We shall use some of the terms used by filmmakers and photographers when discussing their images, since these terms are a handy tool for talking about pictures in a children's book, too.

First Half

The First Half opens with a "long shot" of an empty track, along with text that tells us a train uses the track.

This introduces the "mystery": What is a freight train?

Then we see a series of three "medium shots" of small groups of railcars. The text and pictures together explain the individual parts of a freight train.

The last image in the First Half is a "long shot" of the entire freight train, with the text: "Freight train."

This summarizes and concludes the First Half.

Beginning, middle, end.

Second Half

Now for the Second Half.

It opens with a "long shot" of a moving train along with one word of text: "Moving."

This introduces the subject of the Second Half: *movement*.

Then we see a series of "long shots" showing *where* the train moves, along with text that tells us where (tunnels, cities, trestles).

Next we learn *when* the train moves: night and day.

Finally, the Second Half concludes with text that tells us the train is passing, passing... passed and a "long shot" of the empty track with wisps of smoke from the now-passed freight train.

Once again, we have a beginning, middle and end.

Summary

In *Freight Train*, a seemingly simple story actually has a relatively sophisticated structure.

The writer *crafted* this story carefully. He didn't just split the story into two parts, "definition of freight train" and "movement of freight train" and string together a series of unrelated images. No.

Each half was carefully crafted with a three-part structure. Each half can stand alone as a satisfying whole—not a whole book, of course, but a whole, satisfying segment.

When you combine the two halves and link them together by starting and ending with the same empty track, you've got a powerful story.

Ten, Nine, Eight

by Molly Bang

This is a brilliant, satisfying book!

In this seemingly simple "counting" story about a little girl getting ready for bed, there are two lines of action that draw us through the story to the very end: getting to "1" and going to bed.

In one line of action, we're moving backward from "10" to "1" and in the second line of action, we're moving forward from bath to bed.

What is so satisfying about this book is that the two lines of action reach their resolution simultaneously.

Another reason the story is so satisfying is that it comes full circle, in that it both starts and ends with the protagonist—it starts with the little girl's toes and ends with the little girl tucked in bed.

If we didn't realize at the beginning whose toes these were that were "all washed and warm," we realize it by the end when the little girl is in bed, and we understand that she took a bath before bedtime.

This book also has a two-part structure, as many books do for the very young child.

The first half, from "10" to "6," identifies various things in the little girl's room, while the second half, from "5" to "1," is all about getting ready for bed. Remember, at "5," we now see the little girl in her nightgown.

Also, the second half relates to her relationship with her father—at least most of the pictures do, if not the text. This is yet another reason the story is so satisfying: it shows the warmth and security of a parent's love for his child.

I'll say it again: with all of these elements flawlessly executed, this is a brilliant and satisfying book.

The aspiring children's book writer has much to learn here.

Chicka Chicka Boom Boom

by Bill Martin, Jr., and
John Archambault,
illustrated by Lois Ehlert

In all the excitement of the bright colors and jumble of letters and loud noises and fun sounds (chicka chicka boom boom!), it's easy to overlook the two-part structure of this story, and the perfect circle that is created.

Have a look:

This story starts with a dare! Little lowercase "a" dares "b" to go to the top of the coconut tree. Letter after letter, up they all go. That's part one.

At the midpoint of the story, they all fall down.

In part two, the injured little letters leave the tree one by one and hobble home.

At the very end, in what is essentially a coda, the moon comes out and little "a" starts the story all over again with the same dare and goes back up the coconut tree.

A perfect circle.

Here is what the story looks like in diagram form:

MIDPOINT
Fall
Down

PART I
Go
Up

PART II
Go
Home

Dare
BEGINNING
END

In other stories you'll read about in this book, we talk about certain elements of the story coming full circle, in that a snippet of dialog or a character or an image appears both at the beginning and at the end of a story.

But in this story, *Chicka Chicka Boom Boom*, it's the actual *action* that starts over again and that is why the story *itself* is circular. You can imagine the whole story repeating itself over and over again, day and night! Little "a" is such a rascal!

I am a Bunny

by Ole Risom,
illustrated by Richard Scarry

What a delightful story! As Bunny romps through the wonderland of nature, we share his wonder and joy.

I am a Bunny is also very interesting to the children's book writer for the way it combines a chronological story with the present tense.

The story moves chronologically from spring to summer to fall, then winter—with a circular tie-in to spring again.

However, within each season, Bunny's activities *do not* happen in chronological order. They don't happen in any particular order at all. Bunny uses the present tense to tell us what he does. This present tense implies that his activities happen all the time, at any time, in no particular order.

For example, in summer, Bunny likes to watch birds and frogs, blow dandelion seeds, and huddle under a toadstool when it rains. Since each activity is described in the present tense, we imagine that Bunny engages in these activities whenever he can and in no particular order.

Only at the very end, in winter, does Bunny use a word that signals chronological order. This is when he says, "Then I curl up...."

That word "Then" is the only time he refers to chronological order for his activities.

This would be a very different story if Bunny told his story in chronological fashion.

Look what happens when we just add the word "Then." Reread the story and add for yourself the word "Then" to the beginning of alternate lines, for example, "Then I chase...." "And then I like to watch...." "Then I blow...."

Tied down to a particular order, the activities lose the sense of fun-loving freedom that the unadulterated present tense conveys.

But by combining a chronological story—the march of seasons—with the present tense, we feel the same sense of freedom that Bunny feels.

And since the story is circular and the seasons recur every year, we understand that Bunny enjoys himself this way each and every spring, summer, fall and winter.

Who would think that you could combine a chronological story with the present tense! This is a valuable lesson for the children's book writer.

This technique works with other chronologies that repeat themselves, such as days of the week, months of the year, and year after year.

By combining the circular chronological sequence with the present tense, the reader will understand that the same activities recur in a timeless fashion.

But just because you use the present tense, does not mean your character will have fun.

This is because not all activities are equally fun.

Take the following example written by Melanie Abel especially for this book to show you what I mean:

My Week

My name is Howard.
This is my week.

Monday it's my turn to pour the milk.
It spills.

Tuesday it's my turn to fold clothes.
A sock is missing.

Wednesday it's my turn to set the table.
I can't find enough forks.
Why can't we go out to eat?

Thursday it's my turn to take out the trash. The bag breaks.

Friday it's my turn to feed Woofie.
He slobbers.

Saturday it's my turn to water the garden. The hose leaks. I get wet, too.
Who needs flowers, anyway?

Sunday we all go to church.
I pray for an end to chores.

Then comes Monday....

***

In this example, we understand that these are chores our character does on specific days of the week, each and every week. Alas, he does not have as much fun as Bunny!

But due to the present tense, these activities seem timeless. In fact, the very timelessness of these chores adds an extra measure of burden—in the same way that the timelessness of Bunny's fun activities adds an extra measure of enjoyment.

From *I am a Bunny*, then, the children's book writer learns that by combining a circular chronological sequence with the present tense, the reader will understand that the same activities recur in a timeless fashion.

Goodnight Moon

by Margaret Wise Brown, illustrated by Clement Hurd

In *Goodnight Moon*, before a bunny falls asleep in his "great green room," we say goodnight to objects in his room and outside.

A simple message, but this is by no means a simple book. *Goodnight Moon* has much to teach the children's book writer about the way text and pictures work together to determine the *pace* of a story and to add layers of meaning.

Let us take a look first at the text, then at the pictures, and finally at the interplay of the two.

Pictures

Visually, the book is quite *regular*. The layout alternates between a two-page spread of a long-shot of the room, and two pages of close-ups of individual objects in the room and outside.

Also, the pictures indicate the steady progression of time by showing the bunny's room growing steadily darker.

Text

There are a total of 30 pages of text and/or pictures.

The story itself—the text—has two parts that are somewhat similar in length:

Part I: Identifying objects in the room (70 words), and

Part II: Saying "Goodnight" to objects in the room and outside (60 words).

Part I is a little longer in terms of the number of words. (Even the phrases in Part I are longer.)

Interplay of Text and Pictures: Pacing

In laying out the book, the story aspect of Part II—the text—is stretched like taffy to spread across many more pages than Part I.

Here is what it looks like:

Part I: Identifying objects in the room (70 words **over _eight_ pages**), and

Part II: Saying "Goodnight" to objects in the room and outside (60 words **over _18_ pages**).

The story aspect of Part II is drawn out visually. The pace slows down. We're being lulled to sleep. We're glad that the phrases are shorter and simpler now because as we fall asleep, we can still understand them even though we can't concentrate very well. The text seems to fade to a whisper as we nod off and fall a-s-l-e-e-p.

From *Goodnight Moon*, the children's book writer learns that it is the *interplay* of text and pictures that determines the pace.

Interplay of Text and Pictures: Meaning

The interplay of text and pictures can also add layers of meaning to the story.

Up until the very end of *Goodnight Moon*, there is no difference between what is *said* and what is *shown*. Whenever an object is mentioned in the text, we can follow along and see it in the pictures.

The pictures continue to show us what the text says, up until the very end.

When the text says, "Goodnight stars, Goodnight air," the pictures show us a close-up of the stars which are visible from the bedroom window.

But when the text says, "Goodnight noises everywhere," the picture does not show us "everywhere," as, perhaps, a picture of Earth from outer space would. No. The very last picture returns us to the room with the bunny, secure in his bed.

The *text* takes us out to the world far beyond the bunny's room but the *picture* does not.

This interplay of text and pictures tells us that whatever else is happening in the world, that room is the center of the bunny's universe.

This additional layer of meaning is created because there is a difference between what the text *says* and what the picture *shows*.

Summary

From *Goodnight Moon*, the children's book writer learns that the interplay of text and pictures not only determines the pace, but also is a useful tool for adding layers of meaning to the story.

The Carrot Seed

by Ruth Krauss
illustrated by Crockett Johnson

In *The Carrot Seed*, a young boy plants a carrot seed. Despite the negativity of his family, he perseveres in caring for the seed and in the end, a carrot does, indeed, grow and the boy's faith is vindicated.

What is so striking about *The Carrot Seed* is the *rhythm* created by its simple, repetitive structure.

In fact, the structure of *The Carrot Seed* can best be described using musical notation. I am not a musician, but using my rudimentary knowledge of musical notation, I have illustrated the structure of *The Carrot Seed* on the following page.

In words, here is the structure of *The Carrot Seed*:

1. Whole note (the Set-up):

> *Our main character plants a carrot seed.*

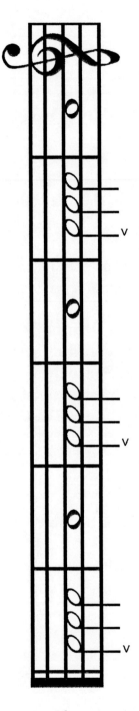

2. Three "beats" of half-notes (Reactions):

His mother is discouraging.

His father is discouraging.

And his big brother is discouraging.
(Accent)

3. Whole note (Character perseveres):

> *Our main character continues to care*
> *for the carrot seed.*

4. Three "beats" of half-notes (the results of Character's efforts):

Success eludes him.

Success eludes him.

Everyone continues to be discouraging.
(Accent)

5. Whole note (Character perseveres):

> *Still our main character continues to*
> *care for the carrot seed.*

6. Three "beats" of half-notes (the Resolution):

Finally,

a carrot comes up

just as our main character knew it would. (Character vindicated / Accent)

Let us look at the structure again, this time in more general terms, and you will see that you can follow the structure of *The Carrot Seed* to create your own stories.

1. The Set-up: a "whole note." Introduce your character and an action or situation that sets into motion a goal to be reached or an outcome to be achieved or a problem to be solved.

2. Three "beats" of reactions to the situation/goal: you can have three different characters—naysayers—pooh-poohing the goal or doubting a positive outcome. Or you can have two characters supporting the goal and the third being the "party-pooper." In either case, your writing should emphasize the third "beat".

3. Your character perseveres: another "whole note."

4. Three "beats" of the goal not being reached or the desired outcome not happening: place an emphasis on the third "beat." Alternatively, write two "beats" of the goal not being

reached and make the third "beat" naysayers telling your character, in effect, "I told you so."

5. Your character perseveres: another "whole note."

6. Three "beats" for the resolution: finally, your character reaches his goal or the desired outcome is achieved. The lesson is learned. The character vindicated. Your writing should emphasize the third "beat."

To prove my point, I gave this structure to writer Melanie Abel and asked her to write a story. She was so enthusiastic, she wrote two. Here is the first one:

Kitten Up a Tree

Little David opened the door and the kitten ran up the tree.

The mailman waved his mail at the kitten and she ran up a little higher. "She won't come down," said the mailman.

The gardener waved his rake at the kitten and she ran up even higher. "She won't come down," said the gardener.

The newsboy waved his newspaper at the kitten and she ran to the highest branch of the tree. "She definitely won't come down," said the newsboy.

Every day little David set out a fresh saucer of milk and sat by the tree.

Monday, Tuesday, Wednesday, the kitten didn't come down.

Thursday, Friday, Saturday, the kitten didn't come down.

Everyone kept saying that she wouldn't come down.

But still little David set out a fresh saucer of milk and sat by the tree.

Then, on Sunday, the kitten inched down the tree and stood in front of David.

And David knew she trusted him.

* * *

As you can see, this follows the structure of *The Carrot Seed* very closely.

Here is a second story by Melanie Abel that follows the same structure, but adds a "coda" at the very end:

Phillip the Fabulous

Phillip is my brother.
Big shot.
He got a set of magic tricks.

Dad said, "You'll be Phillip the
Fabulous."

Mom said, "You'll be Phillip the
Fantastic."

I said, "You'll be Phillip the Failure."

Phillip set out to prove me wrong.

He tried to make a ball float in the air.
It didn't.

He tried to turn his wand into flowers.
It wouldn't.

He tried to turn nickels into dimes.
He couldn't.

Phillip locked himself in his room and
practiced every day.

Then, one day, Phillip came into the
living room in a cape and top hat.
He waved his wand and disappeared.

And he didn't come back.

He never came back.

Dad said, "He's Phillip the Failure."
Mom said, "He's Phillip the Failure."
But I say, "He's Phillip the Fabulous!"

* * *

See how the "coda" repeats the phrasing
used near the beginning? We've come full
circle, which adds a sense of satisfaction and, in
this case, a punch line!

You have seen how *The Carrot Seed*
provides a beautiful example of an elegantly
simple structure that you can use to create an
endless variety of fresh stories.

Seven Blind Mice

by Ed Young

Oh, my! What a multi-layered story!

In this story of seven blind mice solving the mystery of what, exactly, is the "Something" by their pond, there are about as many subplots as there are mice!

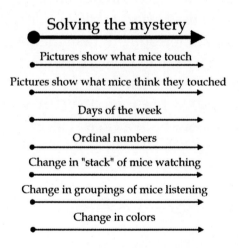

1. Solving the Mystery

The first line of action that draws us through the story is, of course, solving the mystery of what is the "Something."

2. & 3. Two Points of View

As we watch each mouse take his turn to investigate a part of the Something, we see two images of that particular part:

1. a picture of what the mouse *actually* touches (which shows us the part from our own point of view), and

2. a picture of what the mouse *thinks* he touched (which shows us the part from the mouse's point of view).

As you can see, in this book, pictures are used to tell us things that the text does not.

It is interesting to note that each time a mouse reports on the part of the Something that he investigated, that part takes on the same color as the mouse. That is, the Red Mouse reports on a Red Pillar; the Green Mouse reports on a Green Snake, and so on. Talk about being egocentric!

4. Days of the Week

A fourth line of action is the progression of the days of the week.

5. Ordinal Numbers

A fifth line of action is the progression of ordinal numbers: counting first, second, third, etc.

6. Mice Watching

A sixth line of action is the progressive change in the "stack" of mice watching their comrade investigate.

After a mouse has taken his turn investigating, he takes his place at the bottom of the "stack" of mice.

So, for example, after the Red Mouse has taken his turn investigating the Something, he takes his turn at the bottom of the "stack" when Green Mouse goes off to investigate.

7. Mice Listening

A seventh line of action is the progressive change in the groupings of mice listening to the report of their comrade.

Each time a mouse reports on what he thinks he has touched, the other mice listening are aggregated into two groupings:

1. the group that has not yet gone to investigate—and the mouse whose turn it is reports directly to them, and

2. the group to the left that has already investigated the Something and who overhear the report and react among themselves.

With each turn, the first group grows smaller while the second grows larger.

8. Colors

An eighth line of action is the progression of colors of the mice, culminating in the White Mouse—the color white representing the "ultimate" color: when mixing light, all colors together create white—representing, perhaps, the synthesis by the White Mouse of all interpretations of the other mice.

Alternatively, when mixing paints, the absence of color is white—representing, perhaps, the absence of subjectivity that all the other mice exhibit.

To Top It Off

Along with all of these parallel lines of action—parallel subplots—there is also a distinct Beginning, Middle and Ending.

What a story!

"The Tub"
from *George and Martha*

by James Marshall

"The Tub"[1] is one of five quaint stories in *George and Martha* about the big-hearted friendship of two hippos.

"The Tub" is a model of brevity. Take a look:

George was fond of peeking in windows.
[*Picture of George peeking in window*]

One day George peeked in on Martha.
[*Picture of George watching Martha taking a bath*]

He never did *that* again.
"We are friends," said Martha. "But there is such a thing as privacy!"
[*Picture of George with the bathtub over his head and Martha gesturing angrily at him*]

***

Let us extract the main elements of this story. We have:

The Set-up: our character likes to do something.

Middle: our character takes action or something happens to him/her.

Resolution: our character suffers the consequences and learns a lesson.

"The Tub" tells its story in a total of five sentences. Let us take "The Tub" as inspiration and see if it is possible to use these elements to create our own story that is only three sentences long. Set-up, Middle, Resolution: one sentence each. I asked Melanie Abel to try. Here are the two stories that she wrote:

The Ponytail

Andy liked to pull girls' hair...
[*Picture of Andy standing behind a kid with a ponytail and yanking it*]

until he met Spike.
[*Picture showing angry **boy** with ponytail turning around to face a very surprised Andy*]

Andy never pulled hair again.
[*Picture of Andy with black eye and missing tooth*]

Polka Dots

Amanda loved to wear polka dots...
[*Picture of Amanda in polka dotted dress, carrying polka dotted parasol*]

until she got the measles.
[*Picture of Amanda in bed sick with red dots all over her face*]

She never wore polka dots again.
[*Picture of Amanda in striped dress, carrying striped parasol*]

***

Now Melanie Abel was "warmed up." So she challenged herself to write a three-*word* story. Here is what she came up with:

What Goes Up

Up.
[*Picture of a boy tossing a ball up in the air*]

Down.
[*Picture of boy trying to catch the ball as it comes back down toward earth*]

Downer.
[*Picture of disappointed boy watching the ball as it rolls down into a drain; double meaning of "downer" meaning something depressing*]

***

Next, Melanie challenged herself to write a *one-word* story! Here are the results:

The Race

Lickety—
[*Picture of flies in racing jerseys speeding toward finish line*]

splat!
[*Picture of giant fly swatter swatting them*]

***

Pared down to their essentials, what all of the above stories have in common are these elements:
Action
Reaction
Resolution

Try these "minimalist" writing exercises for yourself. Flex your creative muscles. You may find that some of your best ideas are prompted by attempting to write a story that incorporates such limitations in length.

Farmer Duck

by Martin Waddell,
illustrated by Helen Oxenbury

In this story about the beleaguered duck who works the farm while the lazy farmer eats bonbons all day, the author plays with the literary device of anthropomorphism to humorous effect.

In many children's stories that employ anthropomorphism, the animals can do everything that humans can: they think, talk and act like people.

But in *Farmer Duck*, the animals *act* human but they cannot speak like people do—they still sound like the animals that they are: they quack, moo, baa and cluck!

This, of course, is absurd and ludicrous. On the one hand, we are asked to believe that animals can tend the farm like people do, yet we are asked to believe that they cannot speak like people do.

We suspend disbelief to live in a fantasy world, yet a portion of reality intrudes on our fantasy.

By limiting the anthropomorphism, the author has very effectively created *irony* and a delightfully humorous book.

If You Give a Mouse a Cookie

by Laura Joffe Numeroff, illustrated by Felicia Bond

In this story, we're taken on a rollicking ride by the whirlwind antics of one irrepressible mouse.

If You Give a Mouse a Cookie takes three aspects common to most picture storybooks and exaggerates them to their extremes in order to achieve a humorous effect.

Cause and Effect

First of all, most stories have an element of "Cause and Effect." Someone acts and someone else reacts—"*If you give a mouse a cookie, he's going to ask for a glass of milk*"— or someone's own action can lead oneself to react—"*When he looks into the mirror, he might notice his hair needs a trim.*"

In *If You Give a Mouse a Cookie*, the story element of "Cause and Effect" is intentionally emphasized to a ludicrous—and therefore humorous—degree. In fact, the entire story is one long chain of action-reaction-action-reaction-action-reaction....

Irony

Picture books can create irony by having the pictures tell one story while the text tells another.

In addition, within any given picture, we can see characters react differently to the same situation.

In *If You Give a Mouse a Cookie*, we enjoy the irony between the fun-loving, energetic mouse and the exhausted boy who struggles with the chaos that the mouse creates.

In *If You Give a Mouse a Cookie*, the story element of irony is not a one-time occurrence—it is taken to extremes and is created on every page of the book.

Character is Action

In most stories, we learn about the protagonist's character—his personality, qualities and traits—by what he thinks, says and does.

But in *If You Give a Mouse a Cookie*, we get to know the mouse's character almost exclusively by what he *does*. Through his actions, we learn that he is a feisty, frisky and fun-loving mouse. This mouse not only acts, he is hyperactive!

If You Give a Mouse a Cookie takes the story device "Character is Action" and employs it non-stop—in every scene and at every moment of the story—leaving us breathless.

Summary

We have seen how the three story elements, "Cause and Effect," "Irony," and "Character is Action" are each taken to their extremes in *If You Give a Mouse a Cookie*.

Exaggerating any one of these devices would elicit a chuckle, but taken together, the effect is uproarious.

The Snowy Day

by Ezra Jack Keats

The Snowy Day is the gentle story of a boy enjoying the season's first snowfall. The snow may be cold, but the story warms our hearts.

The story is very unusual in that it employs two different plot structures: part of the story is episodic and part is climactic.

The first two-thirds of the story are episodic. There is a string of scenes showing the boy playing in the snow. The incidents are related by theme and character, but not by cause and effect.

Occasionally, within a particular small scene, there is sometimes a climax and resolution. For example, the boy finds a stick, smacks a tree and—plop!—snow falls on his head. Or he climbs up a mountain of snow, reaches the top and then slides down. But notice how each scene is independent and does not build on the previous one.

There is a fairly even emotional keel as we move from scene to scene, and there is no progressive rise in dramatic tension—until we reach the moment when the boy stuffs a snowball in his pocket.

From here on, the plot is progressive. Each scene grows out of the preceding one. The boy undresses, bathes, sleeps, wakes. The order *matters*. One scene follows the next in a progressive fashion. After all, the boy does not bathe before undressing!

The plot structure of the last third of the book can also be described as climactic: tension builds as we wait for the boy to discover that his snowball has melted. Then we are sad for him as he goes to sleep disappointed and happy for him when he joyfully discovers the next morning that fresh snow has fallen.

We experience the emotional highs and lows and highs again associated with a climax and resolution.

The last third of the book also exhibits a three-part structure: Beginning, Middle, Ending.

The Beginning is when the boy puts the snowball in his pocket.

The Middle is when he gets ready for bed.

The climax is when he discovers that the snowball has melted.

The ending relates his bad dream about melting snow and his subsequent delight to discover that new snow has fallen.

If this story had been 100% episodic, it would not have been as satisfying as it is. But the writer was unpredictable and creative, and shifted in the midst of the story to a climactic, progressive, three-part plot structure which creates an emotionally rich experience and a satisfying conclusion.

Part II

Picture Storybooks: The Symmetrical Paradigm

Most picture storybooks are written with a three-act structure. The story moves from a clear Beginning that sets up a problem to be solved, through a Middle having all kinds of obstacles that must be overcome, to an Ending in which the problem is resolved (happily or not). Examples include *Leo the Late Bloomer, Make Way for Ducklings, Corduroy, Where the Wild Things Are, Sylvester and the Magic Pebble* and *Owen.*

Beginning, Middle, End—Act I, Act II, Act III. On the following page you can see what they look like in diagram form.

In this Part of the book, we shall examine in detail the components of the three-act structure, using several favorite children's picture storybooks as examples.

This "fleshed-out" three-act structure, with all of its components specified, I shall call the *Symmetrical Picture Storybook Paradigm.*

Universal Structure

What is so important about the Symmetrical Picture Storybook Paradigm and its

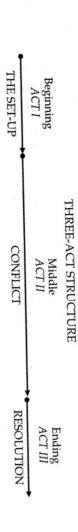

variations is that they can apply to almost *any* plot and *any* sequence of events in a story.

It doesn't matter whether the story is a fairytale, a folktale or any other tale.

It doesn't matter whether the conflict that occurs is person-against-self, person-against-nature, or person-against-person.

It doesn't matter whether the story is told in the first person or third person.

The Symmetrical Picture Storybook Paradigm can apply to most picture storybooks.

Storyspeak: A New Vocabulary

It is important that we use a common language to discuss the elements of the Symmetrical Picture Storybook Paradigm. Until now, no such language—to my knowledge— has been devised for children's picture storybooks. I have therefore taken the initiative to develop one.

The familiar terms used by traditional literary critics fall short of describing the Paradigm. These terms—such as Exposition, Conflict, Rising Action, Climax, Denouement— tell only a part of the story. In fact, they *do not* properly describe the elements of the Paradigm.

Therefore, I have had to look to other disciplines for the vocabulary needed to describe the Paradigm.

Where appropriate, I have borrowed terms from other fields such as screenwriting—after all, the storyboard for a movie bears much resemblance to a children's picture storybook—and coined other terms as needed.

The resemblance of the picture storybook to the movie storyboard is especially striking in such wordless picture books as *Tuesday, Good Night, Gorilla,* and *A Boy, a Dog and a Frog.*

In fact, Uri Shulevitz's book for the aspiring children's picture book writer, *Writing With Pictures: How to Write and Illustrate Children's Books*, is filled with examples that look like stills from animated cartoons.

I have chosen terms from screen*writing* rather than from film criticism or film theory because screen*writing* terms are a better, more practical aid to the writer in the writing process.

For the most part, film criticism and film theory borrow terms from literature and, as I have already said, these terms are insufficient for describing the paradigm.

Screen*writing* terms more accurately describe the parts of the paradigm that the *writer* needs to know in order to *write* his story. These are not necessarily the same terms critics or theorists use to describe a finished work.

If you are not already familiar with terms used by screenwriters, don't worry. Any terms that I have borrowed and adapted from screenwriting are completely explained here.

Anchors

As you will see, the Symmetrical Picture Storybook Paradigm has the following guide-posts or anchors in the story line which I call *Plot Twist I*, *Plot Twist II*, and *Mid-point*.

I shall briefly introduce each anchor below, and following this chapter, I shall explain each anchor in detail as it relates to specific picture storybooks.

Plot Twist I

What sets off the Beginning from the Middle? How do we know that the Beginning is over and the Middle has started?

Something *happens* that serves as punctuation between Act I and Act II. It is an action or event that spins the story off in a new direction. *It is a turning point.*

This punctuation is called *Plot Twist I*.

Plot Twist II

There is a similar punctuation that signals the end of Act II and the start of Act III. It is an action or event *that spins the story off in a new direction. It is the turning point that leads to the resolution.*

This second punctuation is called *Plot Twist II.*

Mid-point

Now let us take a look at the Middle—Act II. What may first appear to be one vast stretch of time filled with various incidents, actually has its own well-defined structure.

In fact, right in the middle of Act II is a pivotal incident that divides Act II into the First Half of Act II and the Second Half of Act II. I call this incident the *Mid-point.*

The First Half of Act II before the Mid-point has its own theme. And the Second Half of Act II has *its own* theme.

The Mid-point both divides Act II into two halves and links the two halves together. Very often, the Mid-point serves to separate *before* and *after.*

With the above in mind, take a look at a more detailed diagram of the three-act structure on the following page.

Highlights of the Paradigm

You can see at a glance from the diagram how nearly *symmetrical* the structure is. This symmetry is a hallmark of the Symmetrical Picture Storybook Paradigm. There are variations, of course, because story-telling is not geometry, after all, but most children's picture storybooks are quite close to being symmetrical.

In particular, Act I is usually very close to being the same length as Act III.

No matter how long or short the story is, Acts I and III *each* make up on average about 20% of the story—again, that is 20% *each*.

In stories that span 27 to 30 pages, this translates into five to seven pages each.

The remainder of the pages—60% of the story—is devoted to Plot Twists I and II and Act II.

Very rarely do you find Act II being shorter than Acts I and III combined.

Also, as illustrated in the diagram, the First Half of Act II is usually about the same

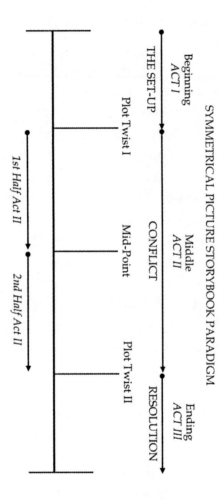

length as the Second Half of Act II. Again: symmetry.

Refinements

The Paradigm has additional refinements called *Pinch I, Pinch II, Mid-spot* and *Coda*. I shall explain each term briefly here, and in the following chapters I shall provide examples of picture storybooks that incorporate these elements.

Pinches I & II

A Pinch is something that happens—an action or event—that keeps the story moving on track. The Pinch propels the story *forward*. It is a moment of punctuation in the story line.

If a story has a Pinch at all, it comes in pairs—Pinch I in Act I and Pinch II in Act III.

Not all storybooks have Pinches. Simple stories such as *Leo the Late Bloomer* and *Harry the Dirty Dog* do not have Pinches.

Examples of more complex picture storybooks that do incorporate Pinches are *Sylvester and the Magic Pebble, Strega Nona, Stone Soup* and *Make Way for Ducklings*.

In *Sylvester and the Magic Pebble* and *Strega Nona*, the Pinches are moments of foreshadowing.

Mid-spot

Whereas the Mid-point is a single incident that takes up only one or two pages, the Mid-spot is an *interlude* in the middle of the story that usually takes up four to five pages.

Examples of picture storybooks with a Mid-spot are *Where the Wild Things Are, Madeline* and *Miss Nelson is Missing!*

To aid us in diagramming such a story, the incident that begins the Mid-spot is called *Mid-point Left* and the incident that ends the Mid-spot is called *Mid-point Right.*

Coda

The Coda is a very short sequence that tells us what happens after the main story line is completed.

Examples of picture storybooks that incorporate a Coda are *Make Way for Ducklings* and *Miss Nelson is Missing!*

Learning from the Best

The best children's book writers may know *intuitively* all of the elements of the Symmetrical Picture Storybook Paradigm, but may not sit down and *consciously* structure their stories with each element and call each element by name.

However, their stories usually incorporate these elements and if we analyze their stories, we are likely to find them.

Once we understand *explicitly* how successful children's stories are structured, we can learn from this how to write our own successful stories.

How to Use Part II of This Book

In this section, I shall diagram for you several celebrated children's picture storybooks so that you can see how these elements are actually implemented.

These analyses are based upon the original books—with the original pictures and pagination—and not on versions that may appear in anthologies which publish abbreviated formats.

These analyses are also based on the page-span of the *story* itself without front or back matter.

To fully appreciate this entire discussion, it is best if you, too, refer to the original books.

Here is an overview of the stories we shall look at in this section and the elements of the Paradigm that they illustrate:

Classic Paradigm:
Leo the Late Bloomer
Harry the Dirty Dog
Corduroy
Good Night, Gorilla

Pinches:
Sylvester and the Magic Pebble
Strega Nona
Stone Soup
Make Way for Ducklings
Madeline

Coda:
Make Way for Ducklings
Miss Nelson is Missing!

Mid-spot:
Where the Wild Things Are
Madeline
Miss Nelson is Missing!

<u>Condensed Paradigm</u>:
"The Letter" from *Frog and Toad are Friends*

Also, we shall examine how the popular storytelling technique of repetition can be incorporated into the Symmetrical Storybook Paradigm by looking at the delightful book *Owen.*

Leo the Late Bloomer

by Robert Kraus,
illustrated by Jose Aruego

To start our investigation of the Symmetrical Picture Storybook Paradigm, we shall look at a very simple story, *Leo the Late Bloomer*, about a youngster who is slow to develop his skills.

Act I

Act I sets up the problem that our main character must solve.

In Act I of *Leo the Late Bloomer*, young Leo can't do anything right.

Plot Twist I

We know that Act I is over and Act II has started when Plot Twist I occurs. Plot Twist I is the first major turning point in the story line.

In *Leo the Late Bloomer*, Plot Twist I is when Leo's mother defines the problem for Leo's father: "Leo is just a late bloomer."

Act II

In Act II, our main character encounters all kinds of difficulties in his effort to solve his problem.

In Act II of _Leo the Late Bloomer_, Leo doesn't bloom, whether he's watched by his father or not.

First Half of Act II

The First Half of Act II, before the Mid-point, has its own theme: it is all about Leo's father watching Leo for signs of blooming.

Mid-point

The _Mid-point_ occurs in the middle of Act II. It is a pivotal incident that divides Act II into the First Half of Act II and the Second Half of Act II. The Mid-point also links the two halves together.

In _Leo the Late Bloomer_, the Mid-point is when Leo's mother cautions his father not to watch Leo anymore because, "A watched bloomer doesn't bloom."

Second Half of Act II

The Second Half of Act II, after the Midpoint, has its own theme: it is all about what happens when Leo's father is *not* watching Leo.

Plot Twist II

Plot Twist II signals the end of Act II and the start of Act III. Plot Twist II is the turning point that leads to the resolution.

In *Leo the Late Bloomer*, it is when Leo blooms.

Act III

In Act III of *Leo the Late Bloomer*, Leo can now do *everything* right!—a happy ending.

Putting It All Together

As you can see, Plot Twist I, the Midpoint and Plot Twist II are the *anchors* in the story line.

Look at the completed diagram of *Leo the Late Bloomer* at the end of this chapter.

You can see at a glance how nearly *symmetrical* the structure is. As said earlier, this is a hallmark of the Symmetrical Picture Storybook Paradigm.

In particular, Act I is the same length as Act III.

And the First Half of Act II is nearly the same length as the Second Half of Act II.

Also, Plot Twist I and Plot Twist II are the same length: two pages each.

Again: symmetry.

Leo the Late Bloomer illustrates the Symmetrical Picture Storybook Paradigm very well.

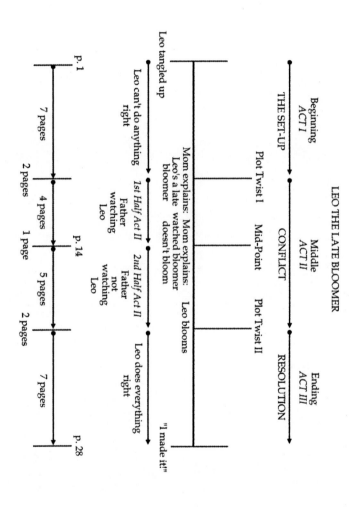

Harry the Dirty Dog

by Gene Zion,
illustrated by Margaret Bloy Graham

Harry the Dirty Dog is the story of a white dog with black spots who doesn't like baths *at all* until he gets so dirty that he turns into a black dog with white spots! To his chagrin, the family he lives with doesn't recognize him, and it is only after he begs them to give him a bath that they realize he is really their Harry, after all.

The story of *Harry the Dirty Dog* actually starts on the title page with the illustration of Harry stealing the scrubbing brush from the bathtub. Therefore, our analysis of the story starts there.

Act I

Act I sets up the problem that our character must solve. In this story, Harry's problem is that he does not like to take a bath.

Plot Twist I

We know that Act I is over and Act II has started when Plot Twist I occurs. Plot Twist I is the first major turning point in the story line.

In *Harry the Dirty Dog*, Plot Twist I is when Harry runs away from home.

Act II

In Act II, our main character encounters all kinds of difficulties as a result of his problem.

In *Harry the Dirty Dog*, Harry learns what it means to get dirty—so dirty that his family doesn't recognize him. He suffers the consequences of not being clean, and only a bath can help him.

First Half of Act II

The First Half of Act II, before the Midpoint, has its own theme: it is all about Harry getting dirty.

Mid-point

The *Mid-point* occurs in the middle of Act II. It is a pivotal incident that divides Act II into the First Half of Act II and the Second Half of Act II. The Mid-point also links the two halves together.

In *Harry the Dirty Dog*, the Mid-point is when Harry runs back home.

Second Half of Act II

The Second Half of Act II, after the Mid-point, has its own theme: it is all about the consequences of being dirty.

Plot Twist II

Plot Twist II signals the end of Act II and the start of Act III. Plot Twist II is the turning point that leads to the resolution.

In *Harry the Dirty Dog*, Plot Twist II is when Harry takes the scrubbing brush upstairs.

Act III

In Act III, Harry overcomes his dislike of baths and actually *begs* to be given one so his family will recognize him. After he is cleaned up, Harry is overjoyed to be welcomed back by his family. Now he appreciates baths so much that he sleeps with his scrubbing brush tucked under his pillow.

Putting It All Together

On the following page is the completed diagram of *Harry the Dirty Dog*.

While the structure of *Harry the Dirty Dog* is not perfectly symmetrical, it is very close!

You can see that the overall structure of *Harry the Dirty Dog* is similar to that of *Leo the Late Bloomer*.

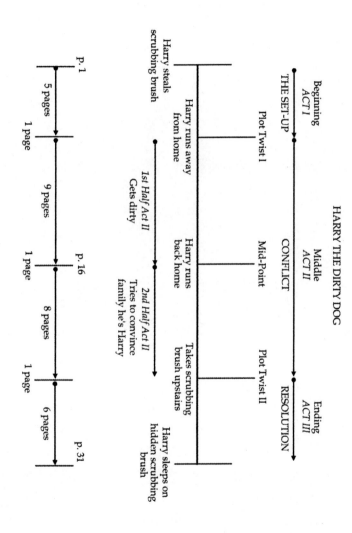

Corduroy

by Don Freeman

Corduroy is the sweet story of a teddy bear waiting on a department store shelf for someone to take him home. Only we, the readers, and the little girl who befriends him, know that he is "real."

Corduroy is another example of a story that follows the Symmetrical Picture Storybook Paradigm.

Act I

Act I sets up the problem that our character must solve. One day, while Corduroy waits for someone to take him home, he overhears someone mention that he is missing a button. From this we understand that Corduroy needs love—and a button.

Plot Twist I

We know that Act I is over and Act II has started when Plot Twist I occurs. Plot Twist I is the first major turning point in the story line.

In *Corduroy*, Plot Twist I is when Corduroy climbs down to search for his button.

Act II

In Act II, our main character encounters all kinds of difficulties in his effort to solve his problem.

In *Corduroy*, Act II is about Corduroy's adventures relating to his search for and discovery of a button.

First Half of Act II

The First Half of Act II, before the Mid-point, has its own theme: it is all about Corduroy's search for his button.

Mid-point

The *Mid-point* occurs in the middle of Act II. It is a pivotal incident that divides Act II into the First Half of Act II and the Second Half of Act II. The Mid-point also links the two halves together.

In *Corduroy*, the Mid-point is when Corduroy finds a button.

Second Half of Act II

The Second Half of Act II, after the Midpoint, has its own theme: it is all about the consequences of finding a button.

Plot Twist II

Plot Twist II signals the end of Act II and the start of Act III. Plot Twist II is the turning point that leads to the resolution.

In *Corduroy*, Plot Twist II is when Corduroy wakes up and sees the little girl, Lisa.

Act III

In Act III, Corduroy finds a friend, a new home and a button. At the end, the little girl who befriends him sees what we, the readers, have known all along: Corduroy is not just a stuffed teddy bear—he is "real."

Putting It All Together

At the end of this chapter is the completed diagram of *Corduroy*.

While the structure of *Corduroy* is not perfectly symmetrical, it is very close!

You can see that the overall structure of *Corduroy* is similar to that of *Leo the Late Bloomer* and *Harry the Dirty Dog*.

Corduroy

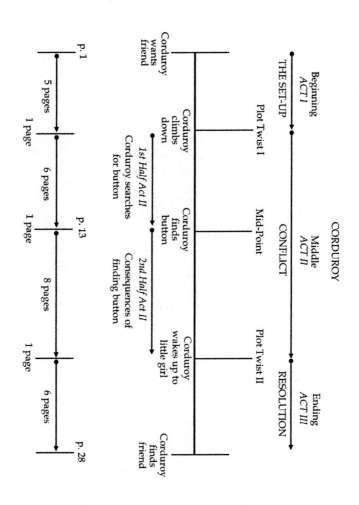

95

Good Night, Gorilla

by Peggy Rathmann

Good Night, Gorilla is the amusing story of a gorilla in a zoo who outsmarts the unwitting Night Watchman and his wife, and winds up sleeping soundly in their bed!

There are almost no words spoken other than "Good night," but what a good time we have!

Even though this story is told almost entirely in pictures, its structure is highly sophisticated and is, in fact, a good example of the Symmetrical Picture Storybook Paradigm.

Act I

Act I sets up the problem that our character faces.

In *Good Night, Gorilla*, the problem is the Night Watchman's. As he says "Good night" to the Gorilla, the Gorilla steals his keys, without the Night Watchman realizing it.

The Gorilla unlocks the door to his cage and lets himself out. Then the Gorilla starts to follow the Night Watchman on his rounds of the zoo.

Plot Twist I

We know that Act I is over and Act II has started when Plot Twist I occurs. Plot Twist I is the first major turning point in the story line.

In *Good Night, Gorilla,* Plot Twist I is when the Gorilla begins to free the other animals from their cages. This happens in two steps.

First, as the Night Watchman and the Gorilla pass the Elephant's cage, we see fore-shadowing of something about to happen when the Gorilla looks back at the Elephant in his cage.

Then, in the very next picture, we understand what that foreshadowing was about when we see the now-free Elephant standing beside the Gorilla in front of the Lion's cage while the Gorilla reaches up to unlock that cage, too.

Act II

In Act II, our main character encounters all kinds of difficulties as a result of his problem.

First Half of Act II

The First Half of Act II, before the Mid-point, has its own theme: it is all about the Night Watchman's reaction—or lack of it—to what is happening.

In the First Half of Act II, the Gorilla opens the cages to all of the animals that the Night Watchman says "Good night" to, and they all trail after him—all the way to his house and even into his bedroom where they settle in for the night!

Mid-point

The *Mid-point* occurs in the middle of Act II. It is a pivotal incident that divides Act II into the First Half of Act II and the Second Half of Act II. The Mid-point also links the two halves together.

In *Good Night, Gorilla,* the Mid-point is when the focus of the story shifts from the Night Watchman to his Wife. This happens when the Night Watchman gets into bed with his back to his Wife, and she says to him, "Good night."

Second Half of Act II

The Second Half of Act II, after the Mid-point, has its own theme: it is all about the Wife's reaction to the animals in the bedroom.

In the Second Half of Act II, after the Wife says "Good night" to her husband, all the animals say "Good night" right back! We see her surprised reaction in wonderfully funny slow-motion.

Then the Wife takes all the animals back to the zoo. She thinks that's the end of it and goes back home.

Plot Twist II

Plot Twist II signals the end of Act II and the start of Act III. Plot Twist II is the turning point that leads to the resolution.

In *Good Night, Gorilla*, Plot Twist II is when the Gorilla, who still has the Night Watchman's keys, now follows the Wife back home!

Act III

In Act III, the Wife doesn't realize that the Gorilla—and his friend, the banana-carrying mouse—have crept back into bed with her, and neither does her husband. Oblivious, the couple say "Good night" to each other and fall asleep.

At the end, the Mouse whispers "Good night, Gorilla"—echoing the very first words of the story—but the Gorilla doesn't hear because he's already sound asleep.

What a great story!

Putting It All Together

On the following page is the completed diagram of *Good Night, Gorilla*. As you can see, even though this story is told almost entirely in pictures, its structure is a good example of the Symmetrical Picture Storybook Paradigm.

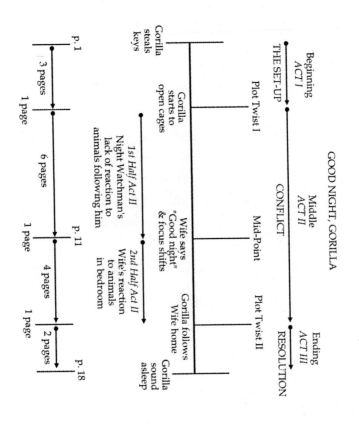

Sylvester and the Magic Pebble

by William Steig

In this touching story, a son and his parents suffer the anguish of separation and long to be reunited.

The trouble begins when Sylvester finds a magic pebble. When he holds it, the pebble grants any wish he makes. Then Sylvester is frightened by seeing a lion, and he wishes he were a rock. He is immediately turned into a rock, but now cannot hold the pebble again in order to wish being turned back to normal.

This story has all the structural elements that *Leo the Late Bloomer* and *Corduroy* have—including Plot Twist I, Mid-point and Plot Twist II—but it also has a new feature: the *Pinch*.

The Pinch is a moment of punctuation that may occur in a story line. It is an action or event that propels the story forward. If a story has a Pinch at all, it comes in pairs—Pinch I in Act I and Pinch II in Act III.

As you will see, in *Sylvester and the Magic Pebble*, Pinch I and Pinch II are moments of *foreshadowing*.

Act I

Act I sets up the problem that our character must solve. In *Sylvester and the Magic Pebble*, the problem is that Sylvester has turned into a rock and cannot return to his normal self.

Pinch I

Within Act I is the moment of punctuation which we have called *Pinch I*. It is an action or event that propels the story forward.

In *Sylvester and the Magic Pebble*, Pinch I occurs when Sylvester makes his first wish and we have a moment of *foreshadowing* of something yet to come. This Pinch adds suspense to Act I.

Plot Twist I

We know that Act I is over and Act II has started when Plot Twist I occurs. Plot Twist I is the first major turning point in the story line.

In *Sylvester and the Magic Pebble*, Plot Twist I occurs when Sylvester is turned into a rock.

Act II

Act II is about Sylvester's parents' life without their beloved son.

First Half of Act II

The First Half of Act II, before the Mid-point, has its own theme: it is all about the parents' search for Sylvester.

Mid-point

The *Mid-point* occurs in the middle of Act II. It is a pivotal incident that divides Act II into the First Half of Act II and the Second Half of Act II.

In *Sylvester and the Magic Pebble*, the Mid-point is when Sylvester's parents give up searching.

Second Half of Act II

The Second Half of Act II, after the Mid-point, has its own theme: it is all about the passage of time with Sylvester as a rock after his parents have given up searching.

Plot Twist II

Plot Twist II signals the end of Act II and the start of Act III. Plot Twist II is the turning point that leads to the resolution.

In *Sylvester and the Magic Pebble*, Plot Twist II is when Sylvester's parents decide to go for a picnic.

Act III

In Act III, Sylvester is turned back into his old self and reunited with his loving parents, who are overjoyed to see him again.

Pinch II

Within Act III is the moment of punctuation which we have called *Pinch II*. It is an action or event that propels the story forward.

In *Sylvester and the Magic Pebble*, Pinch II occurs when Sylvester's father finds the magic pebble and places it on the rock. This is a moment of *foreshadowing* of something about to happen. This Pinch adds suspense to Act III.

Putting It All Together

On the following page is the completed diagram of *Sylvester and the Magic Pebble.*

As you can see, the structure is quite symmetrical, as it is in other stories that we have examined.

Sylvester and the Magic Pebble also shows how Pinch I and Pinch II can be used to add moments of *foreshadowing* that add suspense to Acts I and III.

Symmetrical Picture Storybook Paradigm

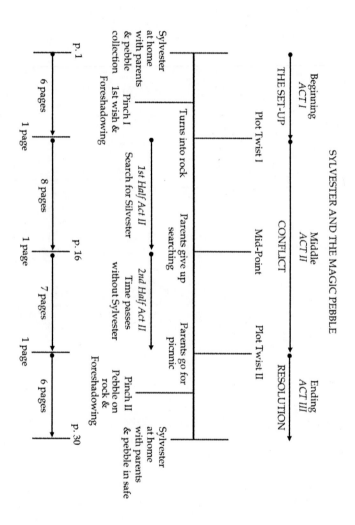

108

Strega Nona

by Tomie de Paola

In this story, a curious fool by the name of Big Anthony takes advantage of Strega Nona the Witch's absence, to try for himself to make her magic pasta pot work.

Big Anthony has overheard the magic chant that makes the pot fill continuously with pasta on its own, but he has missed the key to making the pot *stop* producing pasta, and the pasta overruns the town.

This story is structurally similar to *Sylvester and the Magic Pebble* in that it, too, incorporates the Pinch.

The Pinch is a moment of punctuation that may occur in a story line. It is an action or event that propels the story forward. If a story has a Pinch at all, it comes in pairs—Pinch I in Act I and Pinch II in Act III.

In *Strega Nona*, as in *Sylvester and the Magic Pebble*, Pinch I and Pinch II are moments of *foreshadowing*.

Act I

Act I sets up the problem that our character must overcome. In *Strega Nona*, the problem is that Big Anthony is a fool who wants to meddle with something that does not belong to him.

Pinch I

Within Act I is the moment of punctuation which we have called *Pinch I*. It is an action or event that propels the story forward.

In *Strega Nona*, *Pinch I* occurs when Strega Nona warns Big Anthony not to touch her pasta pot, and we have a moment of *foreshadowing* of something yet to come. This Pinch adds suspense to Act I.

Plot Twist I

We know that Act I is over and Act II has started when Plot Twist I occurs. Plot Twist I is the first major turning point in the story line.

In *Strega Nona*, Plot Twist I occurs when Strega Nona blows three kisses toward the pot and we, the readers, learn that this is the key to making the pot stop producing pasta. Big Anthony, however, does not see this.

Act II

Act II is about what happens when Big Anthony causes the magic pot to fill continuously with pasta all by itself—but cannot stop it.

First Half of Act II

The First Half of Act II, before the Mid-point, has its own theme: it is all about people being happy to see the pot fill continuously with pasta.

Mid-point

The *Mid-point* occurs in the middle of Act II. It is a pivotal incident that divides Act II into the First Half of Act II and the Second Half of Act II. The Mid-point also links the two halves together.

In *Strega Nona*, the Mid-point is when the pasta starts to flow out the door of Strega Nona's house.

Second Half of Act II

The Second Half of Act II, after the Midpoint, has its own theme: it is all about people being unhappy that the pasta is overflowing their town.

Plot Twist II

Plot Twist II signals the end of Act II and the start of Act III. Plot Twist II is the turning point that leads to the resolution.

In _Strega Nona_, Plot Twist II occurs when Strega Nona blows three kisses toward the pasta pot and causes it to stop producing pasta.

Act III

In Act III, Big Anthony is fittingly punished for the trouble he has caused.

Pinch II

Within Act III is the moment of punctuation which we have called _Pinch II_. It is an action or event that propels the story forward.

In *Strega Nona*, Pinch II is when Strega Nona holds out a fork to Big Anthony. This is a moment of *foreshadowing* of something about to happen.

Later we see what this means—that Big Anthony will have to eat all the pasta!

Putting It All Together

On the following page is the completed diagram of *Strega Nona*.

As you can see, the structure is quite symmetrical. *Strega Nona* also shows how Pinch I and Pinch II can be used to add moments of *foreshadowing* to Acts I and III.

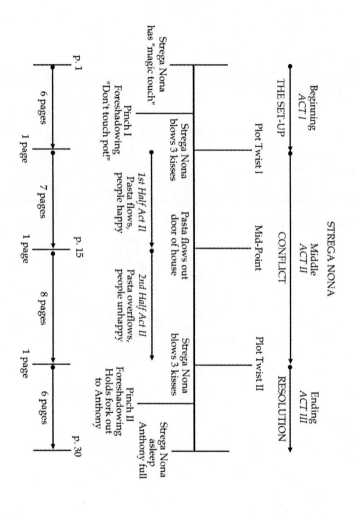

Stone Soup

by Marcia Brown

In this story, three hungry, tired soldiers outwit selfish villagers and beguile them into providing their best food and accommodations.

This story is structurally similar to *Sylvester and the Magic Pebble* and *Strega Nona* in that it, too, incorporates the Pinch.

The Pinch is a moment of punctuation that may occur in a story line. It is an action or event that propels the story forward. If a story has a Pinch at all, it comes in pairs—Pinch I in Act I and Pinch II in Act III.

In *Stone Soup*, Pinch I and Pinch II are moments of *opposites*.

Act I

Act I sets up the problem that our characters must overcome. In *Stone Soup*, the problem is that three hungry, tired soldiers need food to eat and a place to sleep.

Pinch I

Within Act I is the moment of punctuation which we have called *Pinch I*. It is an action or event that propels the story forward.

In *Stone Soup*, Pinch I occurs when the selfish villagers hide their food.

Plot Twist I

We know that Act I is over and Act II has started when Plot Twist I occurs. Plot Twist I is the first major turning point in the story line.

In *Stone Soup*, Plot Twist I occurs when the soldiers announce that they will make stone soup.

Act II

Act II is all about the making of stone soup.

First Half of Act II

The First Half of Act II, before the Midpoint, has its own theme: it is all about setting up the pot and stones for cooking.

Mid-point

The *Mid-point* occurs in the middle of Act II. It is a pivotal incident that divides Act II into the First Half of Act II and the Second Half of Act II. The Mid-point also links the two halves together.

In *Stone Soup*, the Mid-point is when the first villager—at the behest of the soldiers—volunteers to contribute food for the soup and runs to fetch carrots that she had previously hidden.

Second Half of Act II

The Second Half of Act II, after the Mid-point, has its own theme: it is all about the rest of the villagers responding to the soldiers' suggestions by fetching their own hidden food for the soup.

Plot Twist II

Plot Twist II signals the end of Act II and the start of Act III. Plot Twist II is the turning point that leads to the resolution.

In *Stone Soup*, Plot Twist II is when the villagers not only respond to suggestions that the soldiers make, they now take the initiative and suggest bread, a roast and cider for a true banquet.

Act III

In Act III, the villagers are in high spirits. The villagers fete the soldiers with food, wine, dancing, song—and the best beds in the village. The soldiers are treated like royalty and given a royal send-off. The villagers are grateful to the soldiers—without even realizing that the soldiers have tricked them.

Pinch II

Within Act III is the moment of punctuation which we have called *Pinch II*. It is an action or event that propels the story forward.

In *Stone Soup*, Pinch II occurs when the villagers express their gratitude to the soldiers during a heartfelt send-off. This is a moment of *contrast* to Pinch I.

In Pinch I, the villagers are sorry to see the soldiers *come*. In Pinch II, the villagers are sorry to see the soldiers *go*. In the two Pinches, the villagers' feelings are exactly *opposite*.

Pinch I illustrates their feelings *before* knowing the soldiers and Pinch II illustrates their feelings *after* knowing them.

Putting It All Together

On the following page is the completed diagram of *Stone Soup*.

As you can see, the structure is quite symmetrical. *Stone Soup* also shows how Pinch I and Pinch II can be used to add moments of *contrast* to Acts I and III, and to emphasize the difference between *before* and *after*.

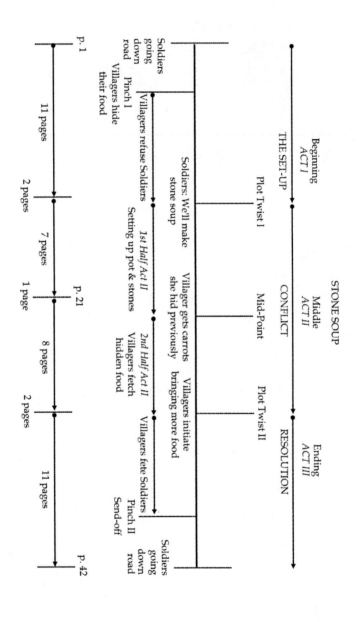

Make Way for Ducklings

by Robert McCloskey

In this story, Mrs. Mallard is determined to find a safe place to care for her babies and to keep them safe as they venture out into the world.

This story is structurally similar to *Sylvester and the Magic Pebble, Strega Nona* and *Stone Soup* in that it, too, incorporates the Pinch.

But *Make Way for Ducklings* has an additional feature, as well: the *Coda*. The Coda is a very short sequence that tells us what happens after the main story line is completed.

Act I

Act I sets up the problem that our characters must overcome. In *Make Way for Ducklings,* the problem is that Mr. and Mrs. Mallard must keep their babies safe. In Act I, they must find a place safe enough to lay their eggs and care for their newly hatched ducklings.

Pinch I

Within Act I is the moment of punctuation which we have called *Pinch I*. It is an action or event that propels the story forward.

In *Make Way for Ducklings*, Pinch I occurs when Mr. and Mrs. Mallard leave the Public Garden because it is not safe enough for babies.

Plot Twist I

We know that Act I is over and Act II has started when Plot Twist I occurs. Plot Twist I is the first major turning point in the story line.

In *Make Way for Ducklings*, Plot Twist I occurs when Mr. and Mrs. Mallard find a suitable place just in time, because they begin to molt and, without their wing feathers, they will be unable to fly.

Act II

Act II is all about experiences in their new home.

First Half of Act II

The First Half of Act II, before the Mid-point, has its own theme: it is all about Mr. and Mrs. Mallard enjoying their new home *together*.

Mid-point

The *Mid-point* occurs in the middle of Act II. It is a pivotal incident that divides Act II into the First Half of Act II and the Second Half of Act II. The Mid-point also links the two halves together.

In *Make Way for Ducklings*, the Mid-point is when Mr. Mallard sets off to explore.

Second Half of Act II

The Second Half of Act II, after the Mid-point, has its own theme: it is all about Mrs. Mallard *alone* teaching her ducklings.

Plot Twist II

Plot Twist II signals the end of Act II and the start of Act III. Plot Twist II is the turning point that leads to the resolution.

In *Make Way for Ducklings*, Plot Twist II is when Mrs. Mallard steps out to cross the road with her ducklings and encounters danger.

Act III

While Act I was all about finding a safe place to lay eggs and teach babies, Act III is all about keeping her ducklings safe as they venture out into the world.

In Act III, Mrs. Mallard must make sure that she and her ducklings safely reach the Public Garden where Mr. Mallard is waiting for them.

Pinch II

Within Act III is the moment of punctuation which we have called *Pinch II*. It is an action or event that propels the story forward.

In *Make Way for Ducklings*, Pinch II is when the Michael the policeman calls for backup so his fellow officers will also help Mrs. Mallard and her ducklings.

Coda

The Coda is a very short sequence that tells us what happens after the main story line is completed.

In *Make Way for Ducklings*, the Coda tells us what happens after Mrs. Mallard and the ducklings arrive safely at the Public Garden and meet Mr. Mallard there.

The Coda tells us that:

"The ducklings liked the Public Garden so much that they decided to live there. All day long they follow the swan boats and eat peanuts. And when night falls they swim to their little island and go to sleep."

Putting It All Together

On the following page is the completed diagram of *Make Way for Ducklings*.

As you can see, the structure is quite symmetrical. *Make Way for Ducklings* also incorporates Pinch I, Pinch II and a Coda.

Symmetrical Picture Storybook Paradigm

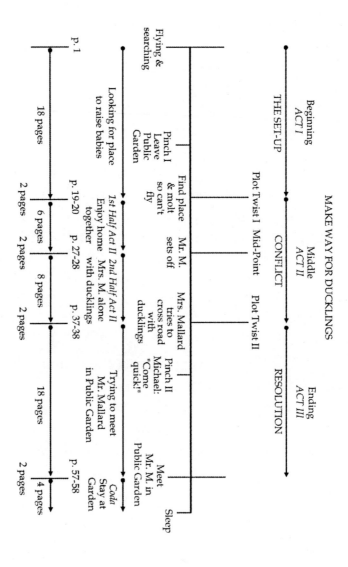

MAKE WAY FOR DUCKLINGS

Where the Wild Things Are

by Maurice Sendak

In this story, young Max is sent to bed without his supper because he has been too wild. From his room, he journeys to the land of the Wild Things and becomes their king. After a wild rumpus there, he tires and misses home. When he returns, he finds his supper waiting for him—and it is still hot.

This story incorporates a structural feature that we have not encountered before: the *Mid-spot*.

The Mid-spot extends the concept of the Mid-point. Whereas the Mid-point is a specific incident in the middle of the story that spans one to two pages, the Mid-spot is an *interlude* in the middle of the story that spans three to five pages.

Act I

Act I sets up the problem that our character must overcome. In *Where the Wild Things Are*, the problem is that Max wants to be wild in spite of being sent to bed without his supper.

Plot Twist I

We know that Act I is over and Act II has started when Plot Twist I occurs. Plot Twist I is the first major turning point in the story line.

In *Where the Wild Things Are*, Plot Twist I occurs when a forest begins to grow in Max's room.

Act II

Act II is all about Max's journey to and experiences in the land of the Wild Things.

First Half of Act II

The First Half of Act II, before the Mid-spot, has its own theme: it is all about Max's journey to the land of the Wild Things.

Mid-spot

The *Mid-spot* occurs in the middle of Act II. It is a pivotal interlude that divides Act II into the First Half of Act II and the Second Half of Act II.

The Mid-spot extends the concept of the Mid-point. Whereas the Mid-point is a specific incident that spans one to two pages, the Mid-spot is an *interlude* in the middle of the story that spans three to five pages.

The incident that begins the Mid-spot is called *Mid-point Left*, and the incident that ends the Mid-spot is called *Mid-point Right*.

In *Where the Wild Things Are*, the Mid-spot is about Max "taming" the Wild Things and being made their king.

The interlude begins when Max lands ashore and meets a crowd of Wild Things (Mid-point Left) and ends when Max is made their king (Mid-point Right).

Second Half of Act II

The Second Half of Act II, after the Mid-spot, has its own theme: it is all about the wild rumpus of Max and the Wild Things.

Plot Twist II

Plot Twist II signals the end of Act II and the start of Act III. Plot Twist II is the turning point that leads to the resolution.

In *Where the Wild Things Are*, Plot Twist II is when Max begins to miss home.

Act III

In Act III, Max sails home and finds his supper waiting for him. From this Max learns that, even though he has been wild, his mother still loves him.

Putting It All Together

On the following page is the completed diagram of *Where the Wild Things Are.*

As you can see, the structure is roughly symmetrical and incorporates two Plot Twists and a Mid-spot.

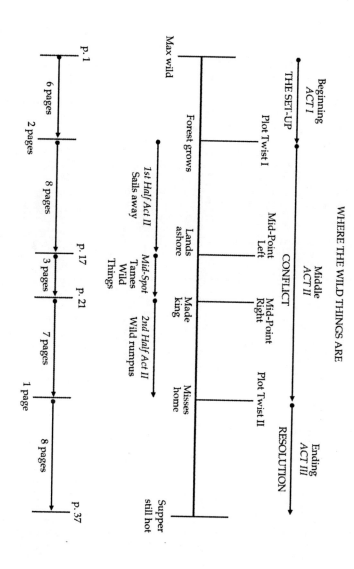

Madeline

by Ludwig Bemelmans

In this story, a high-spirited little girl named Madeline lives in a house with 11 other girls and Miss Clavel. The girls are all expected to conform and do whatever Miss Clavel says. However, Madeline is special. She does not conform. She has a unique personality and unique experiences, and the other girls want to be special, too—just like Madeline.

This story is structurally similar to *Where the Wild Things Are* in that it, too, incorporates a Mid-spot.

The Mid-spot extends the concept of the Mid-point. Whereas the Mid-point is a specific incident in the middle of the story that spans one to two pages, the Mid-spot is an *interlude* in the middle of the story that spans three to five pages.

Madeline is also structurally similar to *Sylvester and the Magic Pebble* in that it incorporates *Pinches*.

A Pinch is a moment of punctuation that may occur in a story line. It is an action or event that propels the story forward. If a story has a Pinch at all, it comes in pairs—Pinch I in Act I and Pinch II in Act III.

Act I

Act I sets up the problem that our characters must overcome. In *Madeline*, the problem is that 12 little girls living under the guidance of Miss Clavel are all expected to be alike.

Pinch I

Within Act I is the moment of punctuation which we have called *Pinch I*. It is an action or event that propels the story forward.

In *Madeline*, Pinch I occurs when the story shifts from the house where the little girls live to scenes showing famous Parisian landmarks.

Plot Twist I

We know that Act I is over and Act II has started when Plot Twist I occurs. Plot Twist I is the first major turning point in the story line.

In *Madeline*, Plot Twist I occurs when we are introduced to Madeline. From the first moment we see her, we know that she is different: at the very least, she is the "smallest."

Act II

Act II is all about how special Madeline is.

First Half of Act II

The First Half of Act II, before the Mid-spot, has its own theme: it is all about Madeline's unique personality—her joie de vivre and fearlessness.

Mid-spot

The *Mid-spot* occurs in the middle of Act II. It is a pivotal interlude that divides Act II into the First Half of Act II and the Second Half of Act II.

The Mid-spot extends the concept of the Mid-point. Whereas the Mid-point is a specific incident that spans one to two pages, the Mid-spot is an *interlude* in the middle of the story that spans three to five pages.

The incident that begins the Mid-spot is called *Mid-point Left*, and the incident that ends the Mid-spot is called *Mid-point Right*.

In *Madeline*, the Mid-spot is about Madeline's special experiences: going to the hospital and her first ten days of convalescence there.

The interlude begins when the doctor says, "...it's an appendix!" (Mid-point Left) and ends with "...so ten days passed quickly by" (Mid-point Right).

Second Half of Act II

The Second Half of Act II, after the Midspot, has its own theme: it is all about the girls visiting Madeline and seeing the special treatment she has received at the hospital: her father has lavished her with gifts.

Plot Twist II

Plot Twist II signals the end of Act II and the start of Act III. Plot Twist II is the turning point that leads to the resolution.

In *Madeline*, Plot Twist II is when Madeline reveals her very impressive scar. This is another way that Madeline is special. Because she had a special illness that the other girls didn't have, she has a special scar that the other girls don't have.

Act III

In Act III, the 11 little girls want to be special—just like Madeline—even if it means having their appendix out!

Pinch II

Within Act III is the moment of punctuation which we have called *Pinch II*. It is an action or event that propels the story forward.

In *Madeline*, Pinch II occurs after the girls have returned home from visiting Madeline and gone to bed. Pinch II is when—for the second time in the story—Miss Clavel awakes in the middle of the night and exclaims, "Something is not right!"

After Pinch II, Miss Clavel races to find out what is wrong and finds the girls boohooing because they want their appendix out, too. At the end, Miss Clavel urges them to "Thank the lord you are well!" and bids them good night.

Putting It All Together

On the following page is the completed diagram of _Madeline._

As you can see, the structure is quite symmetrical and incorporates two Plot Twists, two Pinches, and a Mid-spot.

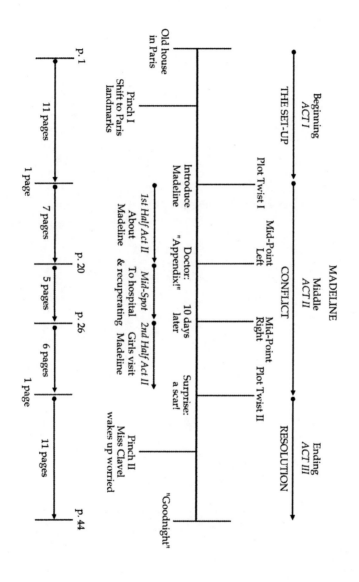

Miss Nelson is Missing!

by Harry Allard,
illustrated by James Marshall

In this story, Miss Nelson, a sweet teacher, is plagued by a classroom-full of misbehaving kids, and decides that "something will have to be done." The next morning, Miss Nelson is replaced by Miss Viola Swamp, who is so onerous that the children actually miss Miss Nelson. When Miss Nelson returns, the children are so happy to see her that they now gladly behave. At the end, we discover that Miss Nelson *is* Miss Swamp and has successfully tricked the kids and taught them a lesson. Now that's a teacher!

This story is structurally similar to *Where the Wild Things Are* and *Madeline* in that it has a Mid-spot, and similar to *Make Way for Ducklings* in that it has a Coda.

Act I

Act I sets up the problem that our character must overcome. In *Miss Nelson is Missing!* the problem is that the kids in Miss Nelson's class misbehave.

141

Plot Twist I

We know that Act I is over and Act II has started when Plot Twist I occurs. Plot Twist I is the first major turning point in the story line.

In *Miss Nelson is Missing!* Plot Twist I occurs when an unpleasant voice hisses at the kids, "Not so fast!"

Act II

Act II is all about the kids missing Miss Nelson.

First Half of Act II

The First Half of Act II, before the Mid-point, has its own theme: it is all about Miss Swamp cracking down on the kids.

Mid-spot

The *Mid-spot* occurs in the middle of Act II. It is a pivotal interlude that divides Act II into the First Half of Act II and the Second Half of Act II.

The Mid-spot extends the concept of the Mid-point. Whereas the Mid-point is a specific incident that spans one to two pages, the Mid-spot is an *interlude* in the middle of the story that spans three to five pages.

The incident that begins the Mid-spot is called *Mid-point Left*, and the incident that ends the Mid-spot is called *Mid-point Right*.

In *Miss Nelson is Missing!* the Mid-spot is about the kids trying to find Miss Nelson.

The interlude begins when the kids go to the police station (Mid-point Left) and ends when the kids see Miss Swamp walking next to Miss Nelson's house (Mid-point Right).

At the police station, the kids talk to Detective McSmogg who "would not be much help" in solving the case of the missing Miss Nelson.

Second Half of Act II

The Second Half of Act II, after the Mid-spot, has its own theme: it is all about the kids guessing what could have happened to Miss Nelson.

Plot Twist II

Plot Twist II signals the end of Act II and the start of Act III. Plot Twist II is the turning point that leads to the resolution.

In *Miss Nelson is Missing!* Plot Twist II is when a sweet voice says to the kids, "Hello, children."

Act III

In Act III, the kids are glad to see Miss Nelson and now behave for her. At the end, we discover that Miss Nelson has masqueraded as Miss Swamp and tricked the kids into behaving.

Coda

The Coda is a very short sequence that tells us what happens after the main story line is completed.

In *Miss Nelson is Missing!* the Coda is about the feckless Detective McSmogg now looking for Miss Swamp.

Putting It All Together

On the following page is the completed diagram of *Miss Nelson is Missing!*

As you can see, the structure is quite symmetrical. *Miss Nelson is Missing!* also incorporates a Mid-spot and a Coda.

Symmetrical Picture Storybook Paradigm

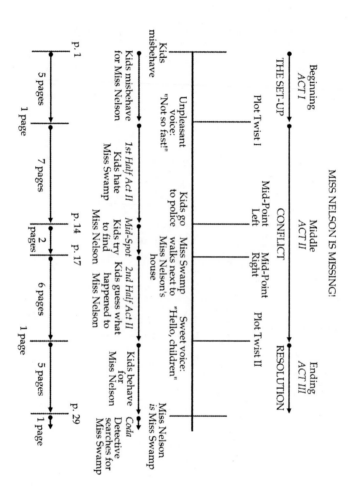

Owen

by Kevin Henkes

In this story, little Owen loves his blanket, Fuzzy, and takes it with him everywhere. The meddling neighbor, Mrs. Tweezers, tells Owen's parents that he is too old for this and gives advice on how to take Fuzzy away from Owen. Yet Owen thwarts his parents' every attempt to take Fuzzy away, until one day his mother comes up with a solution that makes everybody happy.

This story is an action-packed gem squeezed into only 22 pages.

Repetition

Children's picture books are known for their use of repetition. I am including *Owen* in this section to show how repetition can be incorporated into the Symmetrical Storybook Paradigm. In fact, *Owen* does this brilliantly.

And more than that: *Owen* is a superb example of *pacing* for the way it uses repetition without letting the story become tedious.

Act II

In this discussion, we shall concentrate on Act II, where most of the repetition occurs.

Parents Try to Take Fuzzy Away

Between Mrs. Tweezers' first intrusion at Plot Twist I and Owen's mother's idea to solve the problem at Plot Twist II is Act II, in which there are three attempts by Owen's parents to take Fuzzy away from Owen.

Each subsequent attempt is one page *shorter* than the previous one:
- 1st Attempt is three pages long
- 2nd Attempt is two pages long
- 3rd Attempt is one page long

This shortening of each attempt keeps the story from becoming tedious.

Consequences

Each time Owen's parents attempt to take Fuzzy away from him, the consequences are that Owen loves Fuzzy even more. Just as subsequent *attempts* grow shorter in terms of page-length, each *consequence* does, too. Again, this shortening tightens the story and keeps it from becoming tedious.

Mrs. Tweezers' Meddling

Another point of repetition is Mrs. Tweezers' meddling. She appears three times to give her advice: once at Plot Twist I, once plumb in the middle of the story at the Midpoint, and once *before* Plot Twist II. (As we have said, Plot Twist II is when Owen's mother has her bright idea about how to solve the problem.) Mrs. Tweezers appears each time for one page.

Putting It All Together

On the following page is the completed diagram of *Owen*. You can see how *Owen* beautifully incorporates repetition into the Symmetrical Storybook Paradigm, all the while keeping the pacing tight.

Symmetrical Picture Storybook Paradigm

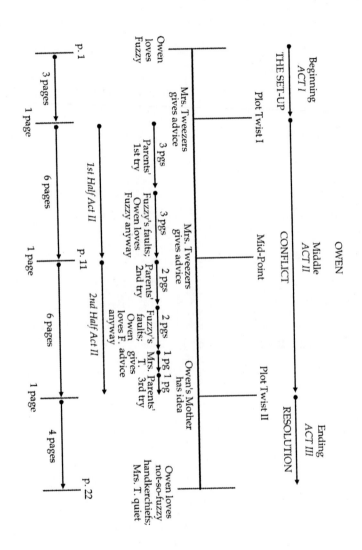

"The Letter" from *Frog and Toad are Friends*

by Arnold Lobel

In this story, Toad is sad because he never receives a letter from anyone. Frog wants to make his friend happy, so he sends Toad a letter himself. In the letter, Frog tells Toad that he is glad that Toad is his best friend. When the letter finally arrives, Toad is very pleased to have it.

I have included this story to show you that even though it is very short—only twelve pages—it follows the Symmetrical Picture Storybook Paradigm quite closely, with the only exception being that Act II is condensed.

Act I

Act I sets up the problem that our characters must overcome. In "The Letter," the problem is that Toad is sad because he never receives a letter from anyone.

Plot Twist I

We know that Act I is over and Act II has started when Plot Twist I occurs. Plot Twist I is the first major turning point in the story line.

In "The Letter," Plot Twist I occurs when Frog rushes home to write Toad a letter. Frog gives it to Snail to deliver.

Act II

Act II is all about Frog trying to get Toad to continue waiting for a letter to arrive.

Since "The Letter" is such a short story, there is no room for the First Half of Act II, the Second Half of Act II and a Mid-point linking the two.

Instead, Act II is one, indivisible block. You might also think of Act II as the Mid-spot.

Plot Twist II

Plot Twist II signals the end of Act II and the start of Act III. Plot Twist II is the turning point that leads to the resolution.

In "The Letter," Plot Twist II is when Frog starts waiting for a letter to arrive. Toad notices and Frog admits that he sent Toad a letter. Frog tells Toad what he wrote and Toad agrees that it makes a very good letter.

Act III

In Act III, Frog and Toad wait for the letter, "feeling happy together," and when Snail finally delivers it, Toad is "very pleased to have it."

Putting It All Together

On the following page is the completed diagram of "The Letter."

As you can see, the structure follows the Symmetrical Picture Storybook Paradigm quite closely, with the only difference being that Act II is condensed.

Symmetrical Picture Storybook Paradigm

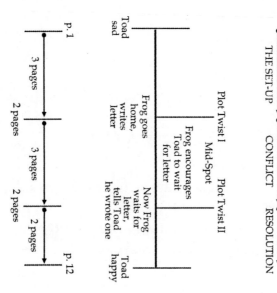

"THE LETTER" FROM FROG AND TOAD ARE FRIENDS

Beginning	Middle	Ending
ACT I	*ACT II*	*ACT III*

THE SET-UP   CONFLICT   RESOLUTION

Plot Twist I   Plot Twist II
Mid-Spot

Toad
sad

Frog goes
home,
writes
letter

Frog encourages
Toad to wait
for letter

Now Frog
waits for
letter,
tells Toad
he wrote one

Toad
happy

p. 1   3 pages   3 pages   2 pages   p. 12

3 pages   2 pages   2 pages

Part III

Picture Storybooks:
The Iterative Paradigm

While most picture storybooks follow the Symmetrical Picture Storybook Paradigm, there is another pattern you should be aware of that appears from time to time which I call the *Iterative Paradigm*.

Page Pattern

You have seen that in the Symmetrical Paradigm the two halves of the story are mirror images of each other. For example, the page pattern might be:

Act I	1st Half Act II	Mid-Point	2nd Half Act II	Act III
3	6	1	6	3

But in the Iterative Paradigm, the page pattern of the second half of the story simply *repeats* the pattern of the first half. In this case, the page pattern might be:

Act I	1st Half Act II	Mid-Point	2nd Half Act II	Act III
3	6	1	3	6

or

Act I	1st Half Act II	Mid-Point	2nd Half Act II	Act III
6	3	1	6	3

Mike Mulligan and His Steam Shovel is an example of a picture storybook that follows the Iterative Paradigm.

Act II

As you can see from the above examples, in the Iterative Paradigm, Act II does not have two *halves* at all. The sections on either side of the Mid-point are not nearly equal in length.

When talking about the Iterative Paradigm, we can more accurately call these two sections the First Part of Act II and the Second Part of Act II.

Mid-Spot

Stories that follow the Iterative Paradigm can also have a Mid-spot instead of a Mid-point. In this case, the page pattern might be:

Act I	1st Part Act II	Mid-Spot	2nd Part Act II	Act III
6	3	4	6	3

Millions of Cats is an example of such a story.

Plot Twists

The Iterative Paradigm also incorporates Plot Twist I and Plot Twist II which we learned about in the Symmetrical Paradigm.

Plot Twist I signals the end of Act I and the beginning of Act II, while Plot Twist II signals the end of Act II and the beginning of Act III.

Other Elements

Further investigation will reveal whether or not the Iterative Paradigm incorporates other structural story elements such as the Pinch and Coda.

Since relatively few stories follow the Iterative Paradigm, it will take some time before enough such stories can be identified to answer this question.

Learning from the Best

In this section, we shall look at two stories that illustrate the Iterative Picture Storybook Paradigm: _Mike Mulligan and His Steam Shovel_ and _Millions of Cats._

Keep in mind that relatively few stories follow the Iterative Paradigm—the Symmetrical Paradigm is much more popular—but nevertheless it is important to understand the structure of such a story because it, too, can be successful.

Mike Mulligan and His Steam Shovel

by Virginia Lee Burton

Mike Mulligan and His Steam Shovel is the story of an outdated steam shovel, Mary Anne, and her proud owner, Mike Mulligan, who meet the challenge of their lifetime in one last hurrah and retire with dignity and satisfaction.

The structure of *Mike Mulligan and His Steam Shovel* is a good example of the Iterative Paradigm.

Act I

Act I sets up the problem that our characters must overcome. In this story, Mike Mulligan and his steam shovel, Mary Anne, are sad that they are being replaced by modern gasoline, electric and diesel shovels.

Plot Twist I

We know that Act I is over and Act II has started when Plot Twist I occurs. Plot

Twist I is the first major turning point in the story line.

In *Mike Mulligan and His Steam Shovel*, Plot Twist I is when Mike and Mary Anne find themselves out of a job.

In spite of their pivotal role in building the urban landscape, Mike and Mary Anne have never actually achieved what Mike has always boasted they could do: dig as much in a day as one hundred men could in a week. And now it seems that they never will because no one will hire them.

Act II

In Act II, our main characters encounter all kinds of difficulties as a result of their problem.

In Act II of *Mike Mulligan and His Steam Shovel*, Mike and Mary Anne journey to the little town of Popperville and try to dig the cellar for the new town hall in record time.

They won't be paid unless they dig the cellar in only one day. If they succeed, it means that they will achieve what they always boasted they could do: dig as much in a day as one hundred men could in a week.

First Part of Act II

The First Part of Act II, before the Mid-point, has its own theme: it is all about Mike and Mary Anne journeying to the little town of Popperville, where the residents are planning to build a new town hall.

Mid-point

In the Iterative Paradigm, the Mid-point occurs in the middle of the entire story, but not necessarily in the middle of Act II. This is because the structure is *not* symmetrical. (Have a look at the diagram at the end of this chapter.)

Nevertheless, the Mid-point is a pivotal incident that divides Act II into the First Part of Act II and the Second Part of Act II. The Mid-point also links the two parts together.

In *Mike Mulligan and His Steam Shovel*, the Mid-point is when Mike convinces the town selectman, Henry B. Swap, to give Mike and Mary Anne a chance to dig the cellar for the town hall.

Mike does this by offering the selectman a deal he can't refuse: if Mike and Mary Anne don't dig the cellar in just one day, they don't have to be paid.

Second Part of Act II

The Second Part of Act II, after the Midpoint, has its own theme: it is all about Mike and Mary Anne's heroic efforts to achieve their goal of digging the cellar in just one day, thereby proving that they can dig as much in a day as one hundred men can in a week.

Plot Twist II

Plot Twist II signals the end of Act II and the start of Act III. Plot Twist II is the turning point that leads to the resolution.

In *Mike Mulligan and His Steam Shovel*, Plot Twist II is when Mike realizes that he and Mary Anne forgot to leave themselves a way to get out of the hole they dug.

Act III

In Act III, one of Popperville's youngest citizens—a little boy who has been watching quietly all day—comes up with the best solution to the problem.

So Mary Anne stays put and lives happily ever after as the furnace in the cellar of the town hall that is built above her. And Mike

Mulligan happily ever after tends to Mary Anne and the building that she keeps warm.

Putting It All Together

On the following page is the completed diagram of *Mike Mulligan and His Steam Shovel*. You can see that it is a good example of the Iterative Paradigm.

The page pattern of the second half of the story simply repeats the pattern of the first half.

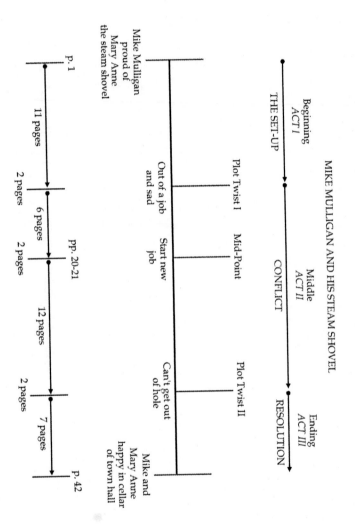

MIKE MULLIGAN AND HIS STEAM SHOVEL

Beginning
ACT I

THE SET-UP

Middle
ACT II

CONFLICT

Ending
ACT III

RESOLUTION

Plot Twist I

Mid-Point

Plot Twist II

Mike Mulligan
proud of
Mary Anne
the steam shovel

Out of a job
and sad

Start new
job

Can't get out
of hole

Mike and
Mary Anne
happy in cellar
of town hall

p. 1

11 pages

2 pages

6 pages

pp. 20–21

2 pages

12 pages

2 pages

7 pages

p. 42

Millions of Cats

by Wanda Gág

Millions of Cats is the story of a very old, lonely couple and their search for the prettiest cat to keep them company—out of the "hundreds of cats, thousands of cats, million and billions and trillions of cats" that they find to choose from.

The structure of *Millions of Cats* is a good example of the Iterative Paradigm that incorporates a Mid-spot.

Act I

Act I sets up the problem that our characters must overcome.

In this story, the very old couple is lonely, and the very old woman longs for a cat to keep them company. Her husband, a very old man, dutifully goes out in search of the prettiest cat.

Plot Twist I

We know that Act I is over and Act II has started when Plot Twist I occurs. Plot

Twist I is the first major turning point in the story line.

In *Millions of Cats*, Plot Twist I is when the very old man sees a hill covered with "hundreds of cats, thousands of cats, million and billions and trillions of cats."

Act II

In Act II, our main character encounters all kinds of difficulties as a result of his problem.

In Act II of *Millions of Cats*, the very old man cannot decide which cat to take home because they are *all* pretty—so he takes them *all* home.

First Part of Act II

The First Part of Act II, before the Midpoint, has its own theme: it is all about the very old man trying to choose the prettiest cat to take home. He selects one after another, until he has chosen them all!

Mid-spot

Whereas the Mid-point is a single incident that takes up only one or two pages, the Mid-spot is an *interlude* in the middle of the story that usually takes up four to five pages.

The Mid-spot is a pivotal interlude that divides Act II into the First Part of Act II and the Second Part of Act II. The Mid-spot also links the two parts together.

In the Iterative Paradigm, the Mid-spot occurs in the middle of the entire story, but not necessarily in the middle of Act II. This is because the structure is *not* symmetrical. (Have a look at the diagram at the end of this chapter.)

In *Millions of Cats*, the Mid-spot is about the very old man's journey home with "hundreds of cats, thousands of cats, million and billions and trillions of cats" and the problems he encounters due to all those cats.

The interlude begins when the very old man sets out for home (Mid-point Left) and ends when the very old man reaches home (Mid-point Right).

Second Part of Act II

The Second Part of Act II, after the Mid-point, has its own theme: it is all about the way only one cat is chosen for the very old couple to keep.

The very old couple wants to keep the prettiest cat, so they ask the cats to decide which one is the prettiest.

A cat fight ensues as all the cats quarrel over which is the prettiest.

Plot Twist II

Plot Twist II signals the end of Act II and the start of Act III. Plot Twist II is the turning point that leads to the resolution.

In *Millions of Cats*, Plot Twist II is when the very old couple venture out after the cat fight and find them all gone except for one thin and scraggly kitten.

Act III

In Act III, the very old couple takes in the kitten and nurtures it, and in time it grows nice and plump—and pretty!

In fact, the very old couple had seen "hundreds of cats, thousands of cats, million and billions and trillions of cats—and not one was as pretty as this one."

Putting It All Together

On the following page is the completed diagram of *Millions of Cats*. You can see that it is a good example of the Iterative Paradigm that incorporates a Mid-spot.

The page pattern of the second half of the story simply repeats the pattern of the first half, with a Mid-spot in the middle.

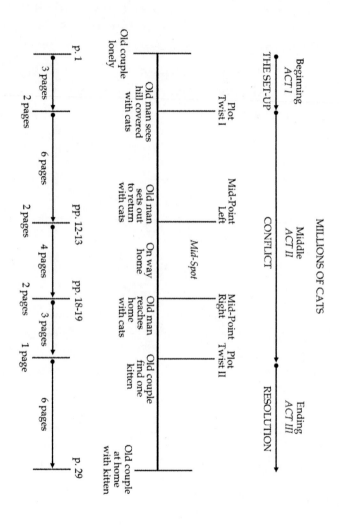

Part IV

Preparing to Write the Picture Storybook

Sometimes, a story may come to you as a gestalt—as a complete whole with all of its interrelated parts—and you have to struggle to write down the story fast enough.

Other times, a story may require you to brainstorm and work bit-by-bit until you see the whole and all of its parts.

In the latter case, this chapter is for you. It will guide you through the steps you need to do to *plan* and *structure* your picture storybook before you sit down to write it.

You will be asked to determine two things: the theme of various stretches of your story and the action or incident that occurs at each anchor in the story line.

You will be asked to *diagram* your story line the way we have in previous chapters.

But here is a surprise: you won't plan your story line in the same order that you read the finished story. Instead, you'll start at both ends and work your way toward the middle.

This chapter will guide you through the process step-by-step, but it assumes that you have already read the discussion on the Symmetrical Picture Storybook Paradigm and that your story will follow this Paradigm, since it is by far the most common form for picture storybooks.

Identifying Themes

You know that you have identified the theme of a stretch of the story line if you can describe it by saying, "this section is all about _____." All of the actions or incidents in that portion of the story are related and can be summed up in one short sentence.

Identifying Story Anchors

When you are planning your story, how do you know when you have hit upon one of the story anchors? What should you look for? Certainly, the action or incident stands out in your mind as being "important." You are likely to be able to identify an action or incident as a story anchor if it involves:

a new scene
a new time
a new location
a new kind of action
a new theme
a new character
a new feeling

a gesture
a warning or foreshadowing

As you can see, one of the hallmarks of a story anchor is that something *new* or *different* has just happened in the story line.

Let's Get Started

Take out some blank sheets of paper. On one sheet, draw a horizontal line across it. That will be the basis of the diagram of your story line—just like the diagrams you saw in previous chapters.

Use the other sheets for writing your notes as you work through the following steps:

Step 1: Define the Problem & the Solution

First, define the problem that your character must solve or overcome and the solution or resolution. State these clearly in one or two sentences.

For example:

The Carrot Seed: A little boy plants a carrot seed. It takes a long time to grow, but in the end it does and the boy's faith is vindicated.

Harry the Dirty Dog: Harry the dog hates baths, until he gets so dirty that the family he lives with doesn't recognize him, so now he *wants* a bath.

Where the Wild Things Are: Young Max is wild and sent to bed without his supper. When he tires of being wild, he finds his supper waiting for him.

Strega Nona: A fool meddles with a witch's magic pasta pot and pasta overruns the village. The fool is taught a lesson by having to eat all the pasta.

Stone Soup: Selfish villagers won't help three hungry, tired soldiers until the soldiers trick them by making "stone soup."

Step 2: Write a Summary

Now that you know the problem and the solution or resolution, write a summary of your story in terms of the main character and his line of action. Your summary should be *short*— three to four sentences.

For example:

The Carrot Seed: A little boy plants a carrot seed. Even though his family keeps telling him that it won't grow, the little boy perseveres in caring for the seed, and in the end, a carrot grows and the boy's faith is vindicated.

Harry the Dirty Dog: This is the story of a dog that doesn't like baths *at all*, so he hides the scrubbing brush and runs away from home. He gets so dirty playing that when he returns, the family he lives with doesn't recognize him. Now Harry *wants* a bath. Once he is clean again and his family realizes that he is really their Harry, after all, he appreciates baths so much that he sleeps with the scrubbing brush under his pillow.

Where the Wild Things Are: In this story, young Max is sent to bed without his supper because he has been too wild. From his room, he journeys to the land of the Wild Things and becomes their king. He plays with the Wild Things until he begins to miss home. When he returns, he finds his supper waiting for him.

Strega Nona: In this story, Big Anthony takes advantage of Strega Nona the Witch's absence, to try for himself to make her magic pasta pot work. Big Anthony gets the pot to work and it fills continuously with pasta on its own, but he can't *stop* the pot from producing pasta and the pasta overruns the town. When Strega Nona returns, she uses her magic to stop the pot and then gives Big Anthony his punishment: to eat all the pasta that has overflowed.

Stone Soup: In this story, three hungry, tired soldiers need food to eat and a place to sleep. When villagers see them approaching, the villagers hide their food. The soldiers decide to outwit the selfish villagers by making "stone soup" and beguile them into providing their best food and accommodations. At the end, the villagers are sorry to see the soldiers go.

Note that the summary is only a *blueprint* for your story. It does not include dialog. It does not determine the point of view or the voice or the tense or anything else about your story. It just defines your main character's problem and the line of action he takes to resolve it.

Step 3: Determine the Theme of Act I

Now that you know what your story is about overall, go back and determine exactly what Act I is about. State it in terms of what your main character is doing.

In *Harry the Dirty Dog*, Act I is about Harry stealing and hiding the scrubbing brush.

In *Where the Wild Things Are*, Act I is about Max causing all kinds of mischief and being sent to bed without his supper.

In *Stone Soup*, Act I is about three hungry, tired soldiers hoping to find food and lodging at the nearby village and the villagers refusing them.

Consider your own story and distill the theme of Act I into a few words and jot it down on your diagram.

Step 4: Determine What the Ending is

The ending is the "goal" of the story. You need to know the ending at the very beginning of the planning process, so you can navigate through your story in such a way that you reach your goal. If you have no clear goal, you will not know how to navigate!

In *Harry the Dirty Dog*, the ending is that Harry appreciates baths so much that he sleeps with his scrubbing brush under his pillow.

In *Where the Wild Things Are*, the ending is that Max finds his supper waiting for him when he returns home—and it is still hot.

In *Stone Soup*, the soldiers depart the village well-fed and well-rested, and the villagers are sorry to see the soldiers go.

Think about your story and describe the ending in one sentence. Then distill the ending into a few words and jot it down on your diagram.

Step 5: Determine What Happens at the First Story Anchor(s)

The first story anchors are Pinch I and Plot Twist II. You have seen in previous chapters that every story has Plot Twist I but not every story has Pinch I.

At the very beginning of the planning process, you may not know if Act I of your story has a Pinch, or not. Don't worry about it. Just write down the salient action or incident that occurs after the beginning of your story. This may turn out to be Pinch I or Plot Twist I.

If the action or incident continues to set up the beginning sequence, you have probably hit upon Pinch I. It occurs in the midst of Act I.

If, however, the action or incident *turns* the story in a new direction, you have hit upon Plot Twist I. It occurs between Act I and Act II.

You may discover that what you first thought was Pinch I actually turns out to be Plot Twist I. That's okay. Be flexible. You will be making adjustments throughout the planning process.

Your story may be so simple—like *Leo the Late Bloomer* or *Harry the Dirty Dog* or *Where the Wild Things Are*—that there is no place for a Pinch.

On the other hand, in *Stone Soup*, for example, there is a Pinch in Act I when the villagers hide their food.

Examples of Plot Twist I in familiar stories include: *Harry the Dirty Dog*, when Harry runs away from home; *Where the Wild Things Are*, when a forest begins to grow in Max's room; and *Stone Soup*, when the soldiers tell the villagers that they (the soldiers) will make "stone soup."

Now think about your own story and describe Pinch I and/or Plot Twist I in terms of your main character and his action. Summarize the story anchor in one phrase or sentence. Distill it to a few words and mark it on your diagram.

If your story has a Pinch in Act I, keep in mind that Pinches come in pairs. So later on, when you get to Act III, you will determine what Pinch II will be.

Step 6: Determine What Happens at the Final Story Anchor(s)

You have already determined what the ending is, so you have the "goal" of your story. Now determine the action or incident at the final story anchor(s) that will lead to your goal.

The final story anchors are Plot Twist II and Pinch II.

Every story has Plot Twist II. It is the *turning* point at the end of Act II that leads to the resolution. It is the action or incident at the end of Act II that turns the story and points it to your "goal," the end.

For example, in *Harry the Dirty Dog*, Plot Twist II is when Harry takes the scrubbing brush up to the bathtub. In *Where the Wild Things Are*, it is when Max begins to miss home. And in *Stone Soup*, it is when the villagers take the initiative and offer their best food for a banquet.

If you had a Pinch in Act I, you will also have a Pinch in Act III called Pinch II. It helps the story move *forward* from Plot Twist II to the end.

For example, in *Stone Soup*, Pinch II is when the villagers express their gratitude to the soldiers during a heartfelt send-off.

If you are having difficulty determining what Pinch II is, take a look again at Pinch I.

If Pinch I is a moment of foreshadowing, perhaps Pinch II is, as well. This is the case in *Sylvester and the Magic Pebble* and *Strega Nona*.

Or, if Pinch I is an action that reveals the character's feelings, perhaps Pinch II expresses an opposite feeling. In this case, the two Pinches taken together would show *before* and *after* feelings. This is the case in *Stone Soup*.

The Pinches do *not* have to be complementary, though, and *Make Way for Ducklings* is an example where they are not.

Now think about your own story and describe Plot Twist II—and Pinch II, too, if needed—in terms of a character and his action. Summarize the story anchor in one phrase or sentence. Distill it to a few words and mark it on your diagram.

Step 7: Describe the Theme of Act III

Look at the stretch of story line that runs from Plot Twist II to the end. This is Act III.

Take a moment to summarize in one phrase or sentence what Act III is about. Identify the theme. Distill your summary to a few words and jot them down on your diagram. Whenever possible, describe Act III in terms of your main character and his action.

For example, in *Harry the Dirty Dog*, Act III is all about Harry getting a bath that he enjoys and his family finally recognizing him. In *Where the Wild Things Are*, it is about Max's journey back home. And in *Stone Soup*, it is about the soldiers being feted by the villagers.

The summary you write now about Act III of your story will help you later, when you actually sit down to write your story. With a clear theme in mind, you will be better able stay on track—and keep your characters on track, too!

Step 8: Determine What Happens at the Mid-point or Mid-spot

Remember, the Mid-point occurs in the middle of Act II. It is a pivotal incident that divides Act II into the First Half of Act II and the Second Half of Act II. It also links the two halves together.

The Mid-spot extends the concept of the Mid-point. Whereas the Mid-point is a specific incident in the middle of the story that spans one to two pages, the Mid-spot is an *interlude* in the middle of the story that spans three to five pages.

As examples, in *Harry the Dirty Dog*, the Mid-point is when Harry runs back home. In *Where the Wild Things Are*, the Mid-spot is when Max tames the Wild Things. And in *Stone Soup*, the Mid-point is when the first villager—at the behest of the soldiers—volunteers to contribute her hidden food for the soup.

Now consider your own story. It may take you some time to determine whether you have a Mid-point or a Mid-spot. But whichever it is, describe it in a sentence or two in terms of a character and his action. Pare it down to a few words and mark it on your diagram.

If you have a Mid-spot, try to determine now how the Mid-spot begins and ends. What action or incident is Mid-point Left and what is

Mid-point Right? Mark them on your diagram, too.

Note:

If your story has Pinches, it is likely to have a Mid-point rather than a Mid-spot.

You probably will not have enough pages left over in a 32-page book to have two Pinches *plus* a Mid-spot.

In fact, two stories with Mid-spots that we have looked at—*Where the Wild Things Are* and *Miss Nelson is Missing!*—do *not* also have Pinches. Only the relatively long (44 pages) *Madeline* has room for two Pinches *plus* a Mid-spot.

Step 9: Describe the Theme of the First Half of Act II

Look at the stretch of story line that runs from Plot Twist I to your Mid-point or Mid-point Left. This stretch is the First Half of Act II. Summarize its theme. What is the First Half of Act II *about*?

Describe it in one phrase or sentence. Whenever possible, describe the theme in terms of your main character and his action.

As examples, in *Harry the Dirty Dog*, the First Half of Act II is all about Harry getting dirty. In *Where the Wild Things Are*, it is all about Max's journey to the land of the Wild Things. And in *Stone Soup*, it is all about setting up the pot and stones for cooking.

Now for you own story, whittle down your description to just a few words and jot it down on your diagram.

Step 10: Describe the Theme of the Second Half of Act II

Look at the stretch of story line that runs from your Mid-point or Mid-point Right to Plot Twist II. This stretch is the Second Half of Act II. Summarize its theme. What is the Second Half of Act II *about?*

For example, in *Harry the Dirty Dog*, the Second Half of Act II is all about Harry trying to convince the family he lives with that, in spite of being dirty, he is still their Harry.

In *Where the Wild Things Are*, the Second Half of Act II is all about the wild rumpus of Max and the Wild Things.

In *Stone Soup*, the Second Half of Act II is all about the rest of the villagers responding to the soldiers' suggestions by fetching their own hidden food for the soup.

Now consider your own story and describe what the Second Half of Act II is about, in terms of a character and his action. Summarize the theme in one phrase or sentence. Then pare down the description to just a few words and jot it down on your diagram.

You're Done!

If you have completed all of the steps above, you now know the following about your story:

- the major problem that your character must solve or overcome
- the solution or resolution to the problem
- Pinch I (optional)
- Plot Twist I
- Mid-point or Mid-spot
- Plot Twist II
- Pinch II (optional)
- Ending
- theme of Act I
- theme of the First Half of Act II
- theme of the Second Half of Act II
- theme of Act III

Now that you have defined the major structural elements of your story, you know the line of action that your main character takes.

You are now ready to begin actually writing your story!

Writing the Story

Now is the time to think about point of view, tense, dialog and so on.

Keep in mind the following guidelines regarding the 32-page book—the most common length for picture storybooks. (Remember: you cannot use all of those 32 pages to tell your story because a few of them are reserved for the front matter.)

Most picture storybooks are symmetrical and Acts I and III *each* take up about 20% of the story. In a 32-page book, that's about five to seven pages *each*.

Plot Points I and II each take up one to two pages.

The Mid-point takes up another one to two pages. Alternatively, a Mid-spot takes up three to five pages.

The First Half of Act II usually takes up five to eight pages, as does the Second Half of Act II.

Analyze Your Finished Story

After you have written your story, lay it out on a storyboard or mockup of a 32-page book. Determine exactly what text goes on each page.

You may discover that your book is better suited to a 24-page spread or a 48-page spread.

In any case, diagram your finished story the way you learned to do in the chapters on the Paradigms, particularly the Symmetrical Paradigm.

See if the story is close to being symmetrical. If it isn't, look at your diagram to determine which sections might be too long or too short. Rewrite your story where necessary.

Appendix

This Appendix provides the raw data used to determine the percentage of story length taken up by Acts I and III in Picture Storybooks employing the Symmetrical Paradigm, as well as graphical representation of this data.

Leo the Late Bloomer
Story length: 28 pages
Act I: 7 pages (25% of story)
Act III: 7 pages (25% of story)

Harry the Dirty Dog
Story length: 31 pages
Act I: 5 pages (16% of story)
Act III: 6 pages (19% of story)

Corduroy
Story length: 28 pages
Act I: 5 pages (18% of story)
Act III: 6 pages (21% of story)

Good Night, Gorilla
Story length: 18 pages
Act I: 3 pages (17% of story)
Act III: 2 pages (11% of story)

Sylvester and the Magic Pebble
Story length: 30 pages
Act I: 6 pages (20% of story)
Act III: 6 pages (20% of story)

Strega Nona
Story length: 30 pages
Act I: 6 pages (20% of story)
Act III: 6 pages (20% of story)

Stone Soup
Story length: 42 pages
Act I: 11 pages (26% of story)
Act III: 11 pages (26% of story)

Make Way for Ducklings
Story length: 58 pages (+ Coda)
Act I: 18 pages (31% of story)
Act III: 18 pages (31% of story)

Where the Wild Things Are
Story length: 37 pages
Act I: 6 pages (16% of story)
Act III: 8 pages (22% of story)

Madeline
Story length: 44 pages
Act I: 11 pages (25% of story)
Act III: 11 pages (25% of story)

Miss Nelson is Missing!
Story length: 29 pages (+ Coda)
Act I: 5 pages (17% of story)
Act III: 5 pages (17% of story)

Owen
Story length: 22 pages
Act I: 3 pages (14% of story)
Act III: 4 pages (18% of story)

"The Letter" from *Frog and Toad Are Friends*
Story length: 12 pages
Act I: 3 pages (25% of story)
Act III: 2 pages (17% of story)

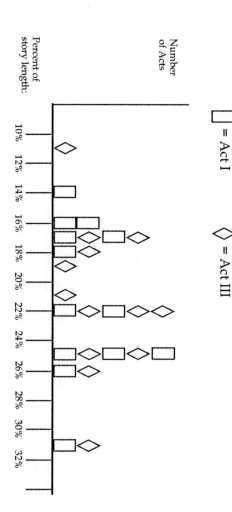

PERCENTAGE OF STORY LENGTH TAKEN UP BY ACT I AND ACT III

- 13 stories, ranging in length from 12 to 58 pages
- Act I and Act III EACH take up an average of 21% of the story length

☐ = Act I

◇ = Act III

Number of Acts

Percent of story length:

10% 12% 14% 16% 18% 20% 22% 24% 26% 28% 30% 32%

Bibliography

The Carrot Seed. Ruth Krauss. Illustrated by Crockett Johnson. Harper, 1945.

Chicka Chicka Boom Boom. Bill Martin, Jr. and John Archambault. Illustrated by Lois Ehlert. Simon & Schuster Books for Young Readers, 1989.

Corduroy. Don Freeman. Viking Press, 1968.

Farmer Duck. Martin Waddell. Illustrated by Helen Oxenbury. Candlewick Press, 1992.

Freight Train. Donald Crews. Greenwillow, 1978.

Good Night, Gorilla. Peggy Rathmann. Putnam, 1994.

Goodnight Moon. Margaret Wise Brown. Illustrated by Clement Hurd. Harper, 1947.

Harry the Dirty Dog. Gene Zion. Illustrated by Margaret Bloy Graham. Harper, 1956.

I am a Bunny. Ole Risom. Illustrated by Richard Scarry. Golden Books, 1963.

If You Give a Mouse a Cookie. Laura Joffee Numeroff. Illustrated by Felicia Bond. Harper & Row, 1985.

R ✓ *Leo the Late Bloomer*. Robert Kraus. Illustrated by Jose Aruego. Windmill Books, 1971.

"The Letter" from *Frog and Toad are Friends*. Arnold Lobel. Harper & Row, 1970.

Madeline. Ludwig Bemelmans. Simon & Schuster, 1939.

Make Way for Ducklings. Robert McCloskey. Viking Press, 1941.

Mike Mulligan and His Steam Shovel. Virginia Lee Burton. Houghton Mifflin, 1939.

R ✓ *Millions of Cats*. Wanda Gág. Coward-McCann, 1928.

Miss Nelson is Missing! Harry Allard. Illustrated by James Marshall. Houghton Mifflin, 1977.

Owen. Kevin Henkes. Greenwillow, 1993.

The Screenwriter's Workbook. Syd Field. Dell, 1984.

Seven Blind Mice. Ed Young. Philomel Books, 1992.

The Snowy Day. Ezra Jack Keats. Viking Press, 1962. ✓ R

Stone Soup. Marcia Brown. Scribner, 1947.

Strega Nona. Tomie de Paola. Prentice-Hall, 1975.

Sylvester and the Magic Pebble. William Steig. Windmill Books, 1969.

Ten, Nine, Eight. Molly Bang. Greenwillow, 1983.

"The Tub" from ***George and Martha***. James Marshall. Houghton Mifflin, 1972.

The Very Hungry Caterpillar. Eric Carle. ✓ R Philomel Books, 1979.

Where the Wild Things Are. Maurice ✓ R Sendak. Harper & Row, 1963.

Writing with Pictures: How to Write and Illustrate Children's Books. Uri Shulevitz. Watson-Guptill, 1985.

Index

Anchor, 69, 176, 181, 183

Carrot Seed, The, 3, 7, 35, 38, 40, 42, 177, 178, 197

Chicka Chicka Boom Boom, 3, 7, 25, 26, 197

Coda, 73, 74, 76, 121, 125, 141, 144, 145, 160, 194, 195

Corduroy, 3, 7, 65, 76, 91, 92, 93, 94, 103, 193, 197

Farmer Duck, 7, 53, 197

Field, Syd, 199

Freight Train, 7, 19, 21, 197

Frog and Toad are Friends, 8, 77, 151, 198

George and Martha, 7, 47, 199

Good Night, Gorilla, 3, 7, 68, 76, 97, 98, 99, 100, 101, 193, 197

Goodnight Moon, 7, 31, 33, 34, 197

Harry the Dirty Dog, 7, 73, 76, 85, 86, 87, 88, 94, 177, 178, 180, 181, 182, 183, 185, 186, 187, 188, 193, 197

I am a Bunny, 7, 27, 30, 197

If You Give a Mouse a Cookie, 7, 55, 56, 57, 198

Iterative Paradigm, 160

Leo the Late Bloomer, 7, 65, 73, 76, 79, 80, 81, 82, 88, 94, 103, 182, 193, 198

Madeline, 8, 74, 76, 133, 134, 135, 136, 137, 138, 141, 187, 194, 198

Make Way for Ducklings, 8, 65, 73, 74, 76, 121, 122, 123, 124, 125, 141, 184, 194, 198

Mid-point, 69, 70, 74, 80, 81, 86, 87, 92, 93, 99, 100, 103, 105, 111, 112, 116, 117, 123, 127, 129, 133, 135, 136, 142, 143, 149, 152, 158, 159, 163, 164, 168, 169, 185, 186, 187, 188, 189, 190

Mid-point Left, 74, 129, 136, 143, 169, 186, 187

Mid-point Right, 74, 129, 136, 143, 169, 186, 188

Mid-point, 80

Mid-spot, 73, 74, 76, 127, 128, 129, 130, 133, 135, 136, 138, 141, 142, 143, 145, 152, 159, 167, 169, 171, 185, 186, 187, 189, 190

Mike Mulligan and His Steam Shovel, 8, 158, 160, 161, 162, 163, 164, 165, 198

Millions of Cats, 8, 159, 160, 167, 168, 169, 170, 171, 198

Miss Nelson is Missing, 8, 74, 76, 141, 142, 143, 144, 145, 187, 195, 198

Owen, 8, 65, 77, 147, 148, 149, 195, 198

Pinch, 73, 74, 76, 103,
104, 106, 107, 109,
110, 112, 113, 115, 116,
118, 119, 121, 122, 124,
125, 133, 134, 137, 138,
160, 181, 182, 183,
184, 187, 189
Pinch I, 73, 103, 104, 106,
107, 109, 110, 112, 113,
115, 116, 118, 119, 122,
124, 125, 133, 134, 137,
181, 182, 183, 184, 189
Pinch II, 73, 103, 106,
107, 109, 112, 113, 115,
118, 119, 124, 125, 133,
137, 183, 184, 189
Plot Twist I, 69, 70, 79,
81, 82, 86, 87, 91, 92,
93, 98, 100, 103, 104,
106, 110, 112, 116, 117,
122, 123, 124, 128, 129,
134, 136, 137, 142, 144,
148, 149, 152, 159, 161,
162, 164, 167, 168, 170,
181, 182, 183, 184, 185,
187, 188, 189
Plot Twist II, 69, 70, 81,
82, 87, 93, 100, 103,
106, 112, 117, 123, 124,
129, 136, 137, 144, 148,
149, 152, 159, 164, 170,
181, 183, 184, 185,
188, 189
Screenwriting, 68
Seven Blind Mice, 7, 43,
199

Shulevitz, Uri, 68, 200
Snowy Day, The, 7, 59,
199
Stone Soup, 8, 73, 76,
115, 116, 117, 118, 119,
121, 178, 179, 180, 181,
182, 184, 185, 186,
187, 188, 194, 199
Strega Nona, 8, 73, 74,
76, 109, 110, 111, 112,
113, 115, 121, 178, 179,
184, 194, 199
Structure, 10, 12, 65
Sylvester and the Magic
Pebble, 3, 7, 65, 73, 74,
76, 103, 104, 105, 106,
107, 109, 115, 121, 133,
184, 194, 199
Symmetrical Paradigm,
10, 11, 65, 67, 69, 71,
75, 79, 82, 91, 97, 101,
151, 153, 157, 175
Ten, Nine, Eight, 7, 23,
79, 85, 97, 199
Very Hungry
Caterpillar, The, 3, 7,
17, 199
Where the Wild Things
Are, 3, 8, 65, 74, 76,
127, 128, 129, 130, 133,
141, 178, 179, 180, 181,
182, 184, 185, 186,
187, 188, 194, 199
Writing with Pictures,
200

About the Author

Eve Heidi Bine-Stock is the Publisher of **E & E Publishing**, which specializes in producing the highest-quality children's picture books.

She is also the author and illustrator, under pseudonym, of numerous books for children.

Printed in the United States
28559LVS00005B/154-171